THE BOOK THAT'S MORE THAN JUST A BOOK - BOOK

THE
BOOK
THAT'S MORE
THAN JUST A
BOOK-
BOOK

PETER KAY

First published in Great Britain in 2011 by Hodder & Stoughton
An Hachette UK company

A CIP catalogue record for this title is available from the British Library

Hardback ISBN 978 1 444 73381 5
Trade Paperback ISBN 978 1 444 73382 2
eBook ISBN 978 1 444 73383 9

Design by James Edgar

Artwork by Lee Acaster and Clifford Webb

Printed and bound in Germany by Mohn media

Hodd   atural,
renewa   grown
in sust   ocesses
are ex   ons of

Writing this is an effort. Now I know those are probably not the words you want to read at the start of a book, but once I start I'm fine. See, I'm only a few lines in and already the cogs are slowly starting to turn.

My problem is that I still associate any kind of written work with the feelings I had towards the homework I used to get at school. The nuns would set us our homework every Friday. Maths, usually. Always algebra for some reason. A form of calculus that, contrary to what the nuns told us, has never once proved useful in any way, shape or form. $5x + 3b = 7z$: what a load of old bollocks – as if life wasn't complicated enough.

We were encouraged to do our homework as soon as we got home on a Friday evening, so that we could have the rest of the weekend to ourselves. This was a logical idea until you then discovered it was five to five and you were up against Crackerjack (go on, shout it).* Algebra didn't stand a chance against Stu Francis and The Krankies, and rightly so.

I have to confess the remainder of the homework would lie unfinished on the breakfast bar, next to the library adjacent to the ballroom … Sorry … I've lost my mind … until that sudden realisation the following Monday morning.

It would then usually be frantically copied from a mate's exercise book in the corridor outside the Maths room. His name was Rob Candy (seriously, that was his name). He was a clever lad who sported a glass eye on the left side of his face – the result of a rather racy game of conkers in top infants. And it was on the left side of his face where I sat, permanently perched during every complicated academic lesson. Boldly copying anything and everything I needed from his exercise book.

We were inseparable – well, we were until he spun round completely unexpectedly when Cath Lowther burnt her stupid tongue whilst licking a nine-volt battery. That's when he discovered what I was up to and with our friendship nothing more than a sham he silently packed up his books and moved to the front of the class, leaving me to fail spectacularly in my solo attempt to construct a disco rope light. I got a grade 'U' in my Electronics GSCE and was later informed that the only questions I'd successfully completed on the exam paper were my name and age. I've never been to a disco since.

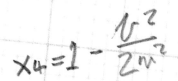

* Now there's a reference lost on a generation; possibly even two … actually maybe even three.

$$Ax^2 + 2Bxy + C\cancel{y^2}$$
$$+ 2Dx + 2Ey + F = 0$$

$$x4 = \frac{1 - v^2}{2u^2}$$

$$5x + 3b = 7z$$

$$\left(\frac{\pi}{3}\right) \quad \frac{\pi}{2} \quad y4 = -1 \sqrt{\left(\frac{v}{u} - \frac{v^2}{2u^2}\right)\left(\frac{v}{u} + \frac{v^2}{2u^2}\right)}$$

$$5x + 3b = \underline{\quad}ks!$$

$$\text{alum}(n) = \frac{710}{r^2} + \Pi$$

Rob Candy is a

It's very different these days – our quota of homework back then was tiny in comparison to what the children of today are expected to complete, and on a nightly basis. I don't know what the teachers do all day, and I don't know who they think they are setting the homework for, because most of the time it's certainly not the children. I was forced to build a replica of a mosque the other week from papier mâché. After an hour on the job I noticed I was alone in the kitchen, my arms draped in soggy sections of AutoMart whilst my son was laid on the couch in the front room watching Nanny McPhee and The Big Bang on pay-per-view. Then he strolls into school on the Monday with a mosque under his arm and takes all the credit. Charming.

Now, in order for this relationship to work, I have to be honest with you. You've bought this book, so technically I like to think of you as my employer. Well, unless of course you've just borrowed it, or, worse still, you're stood reading it in the supermarket. If that's the case you can stick your job up your arse. I wish I'd thrown a sicky now.

SHERGAR

PVA ADHESIVE

Internal use • Dries fast • Dries clear

Throwing a sicky is a dying art. In fact people don't even bother to phone in sick any more; they just text in sick. 'Hi, been up all night, it's coming out of both ends', then press send and job done. In my day there was no such thing as texts; they were just dreams like low-fat best butter and hover boards.★ In my day if you wanted to throw a sicky from work you had two choices. You could either phone in work early and tell the cleaner to tell your manager you were ill, which was always my preference, or you could speak to the manager yourself, but then that meant you'd have to be prepared to do your sick voice and that could often prove awkward.

In fact it was downright ridiculous, the more I think about it. God forbid you'd have just rung up and told him you were sick in a normal voice like a grown-up. Not a chance, it had to be the sick voice. This usually involved me being positioned doubled over in the hall, clutching the phone with one hand and the wall with my other, as I desperately tried to convey the level of my pretend illness via the degree of my acting ability.

★ What? You mean they do exist?

In fact I consider my sick voice to be amongst some of my finest acting work – it's right up there with Brian Potter and that baddy I did in Doctor Who.

I would have to get really psyched up, bend over, squint my eyes and put on this horrible fake dying voice, which sounded like a cross between Ray Winstone and Yoda.

'Hiya, it's Peter [cough, cough]. I sound awful don't I? I said yesterday that I didn't feel well, do you remember?' Bit of reverse psychology, as I strategically attempted to plant the seed the previous day by telling everyman and his dog that I felt dizzy and was starting to feel under the weather, saying things like, 'Is it hot in here or is it me?' (Who else could it be?) They'd reassure me with that clichéd phrase that there was indeed 'a bug going around'. When isn't there?

I'd continue the conversation with my manager. 'I feel really … [cough, cough] … poorly, I think it's one of them twenty-four-hour things [wink, wink].' Just setting my stall out with him. There was no point laying it on too thick by saying I'd had a stroke or something like that. You'd have to follow that up for weeks, months even. Staggering around work, pretending your face was all limp down one side and slurring your words. Thinking 'Christ, what did I say a stroke for? I only wanted the day off.'

If I ever wanted a week off I used to tell work that a member of my family had died. I know that sounds awful on reflection, but I always chose a member of my family I didn't really like. My uncle Nobhead died four times when I was working at Netto. Then the dickhead turned up to do his big shop and I was suspended for dealing in the occult.

Sometimes the manager would unexpectedly say something like, 'Well, if you feel better, will you be in after lunch?' Catching me off guard like that could have me on the ropes if I wasn't prepared. 'Er … well, um … can I see how I am? I'll call you later.' CALL YOU LATER? NO! What was I thinking? Why would I go and say something like that? Now I couldn't enjoy my day off knowing that I had to ring him back after Loose Women and go through the same rigmarole all over again.

Phoning in with a sick voice could occasionally have its downside – like if I gave too good a performance I'd actually start feeling genuinely ill and then the next thing I knew I'd be laid out under a duvet on the couch, eating a bowl of chicken soup and asking people to get me things, like I was at death's door.

'Could you just pass me the remote?'
'Could you get me a brew?'
'Could you just give me a bed bath?'

I once convinced myself I was ill after watching Dr Chris Steele on This Morning, and it wasn't too long before I was examining myself for lumps. I feel I must come clean, like a lot of men I too suffer from hypochondria. I can't just have something a little bit wrong, it's got to be life or death, and in my case it's usually the latter. Like the time I glimpsed red peppers in my poo and thought my days were numbered.

I had something in my eye a few weeks ago but you'd have sworn I was in the early stages of cataracts the way I was behaving. I ended up Googling my symptoms on t'internet. Word of advice, never do that. Talk about opening up a can of worms. I scrolled down the screen and happened to glance at the word 'tumour'. Well, that was it, the next thing I knew I had my local priest on the phone and was asking him to pop round and give me the last rites. I swear I could actually feel the tumour growing in my eye. I could feel it every time I blinked; it was like a grape. (Why do people feel the need to measure tumours in sizes of fruit? This has always baffled me.★)

I was a basket case, pleading with my wife. 'Kiss the kids for me, because Daddy isn't going to see the morning.' Then I sneezed and I realised it was just an eyelash. An eyelash!! After all that, talk about a relief. I felt like Scrooge when he wakes up on Christmas morning, dancing round the kitchen with my new-found lease of life, promising myself that I would never, ever worry like that again. Until three weeks later I tripped up going to the toilet in the middle of the night and found myself sprawled out in the darkness on the bedroom floor. Well, you'd have thought I was Christopher Reeve the way I was carrying on. Calling out to my wife,

★ It was the size of a tangerine. It was like a grapefruit.

I shouted, **'HELP! HELP ME LOVE! I CAN'T FEEL ME LEGS! I CAN'T FEEL ANYTHING FROM THE NECK DOWN'.**

'JUST GET UP, PETER'

was her disinterested, mumbled response.

What upset me was that it was really her fault I was down there having gone arse over tit on a pair of her shoes. Why can't she pick them up? It drives me mad. She comes in and kicks them off, like she's Purdey from The New Avengers with her high kicks. Then wherever they land, that's it; they stay there for days, sometimes months, until I fall over them. That's just what you want in the middle of the night, the heel of a stiletto embedded in the sole of your bare foot. I mean, God forbid she'd pick them up and put them away.

I said to her,

'IF YOU HAPPEN TO SEE ANY OF YOUR SHOES ON THE FLOOR, WHATEVER YOU DO PLEASE DON'T PICK THEM UP – JUST STEP OVER THEM BECAUSE I ENJOY BREAKING MY NECK AT FOUR IN THE MORNING WHEN I GO FOR A PISS.'

Unfortunately my sarcasm was lost on her.

I think I'm going to have to invest in a pair of night-vision goggles because it's like a round from Total Wipeout trying to take a slash in our house in the middle of the night. In fact I'd sooner piss all over myself than stagger around in the dark, stepping on Lego Duplo and discarded coat hangers.

I'm no good with needles and I've become worse as I've got older – that's why I've stopped shooting up.

I can't stand injections and I'll do almost anything to avoid going to the dentist in case they tell me I've got to have a filling. Which is bizarre as I've already got a load of fillings. In fact the back of my mouth looks like a piano if you catch me yawning at the opera. I blame all that Rola Cola my mum forced me to drink as a child.

I'd sue them if they still existed. And I'm still thinking of suing Quality Street for causing me to lose a filling on a Toffee Penny last summer. Be warned! What a palaver that was; I was chewing during Silent Witness and out it popped. I spat it back into the gold Toffee Penny wrapper and stuck it in a bowl on top of the fridge for the court hearing. 'Exhibit A, your honour, I rest my case.'

Even though I looked like a farmer, I left the gap in my tooth for fear of having to face the dentist and, ultimately, his needle. What a stupid boy. I could feel something wasn't right with my tooth. I was becoming more and more sensitive and things finally came to a head when I sucked on a Slush Puppie at Thomas Land and almost toppled off Cranky the Crane had I not been strapped in so securely.

I was in agony all the way home, which wasn't helped by having four under-5s and my sister-in-law in the back of my Seat Alhambra. Then, as I drove up to the toll booth on the M6, things went from bad to worse. Knowing I had the right change, I pulled up to the automatic paying toll as opposed to one that was manned. I wound down the window, threw my £4.80 into the huge collection bucket that they have attached to the side of the paying booth and missed. Don't ask me how or why I missed, I just did.

I sat there open-mouthed. How could I miss? It was a metre wide and I was less than a foot away. According to the computerised total, only £3.80 had gone in and one of the pound coins had bounced out and rolled off under the car. 'FLIPPIN ECK!' (Well, I was in earshot of four pre-schoolers.)

By this time my tooth was really throbbing. I frantically searched for more change that I knew I didn't have. I was hoping it might just magically appear as I opened a selection of compartments on the dashboard, some of which I didn't even know existed until that moment. 'Oh, that would have come in handy for my Opal Fruits,' I thought to myself as I felt down the side of the door.

Helpless and in agony, I was left with no other choice but to get the pound coin out from under the car. I couldn't turn to a member of staff, as the booth was automatic, and anyway there wasn't one to be seen. I couldn't drive forward as the barrier was down. I looked in my rear-view mirror. A queue of cars was gathering behind me. Now panicking and with the sound of 'Hot Potato' by The Wiggles in my ears (a firm favourite with my sister-in-law), I started to open the door. The car was parked so close to the toll that the door had very little room to open. Carefully, painfully, I tried to manoeuvre myself out of the vehicle, a bit like you do when you park in a tight space in the supermarket car park and then notice there's someone sat in the car next to you. Politely you have to make a show of getting out slowly, instead of twatting your door on the side of their car like you would if they hadn't been there.

With very little room, and being a gentleman of the bigger-boned variety,

I attempted to slip down on to my knees in order to blindly feel underneath the car for the elusive pound coin. This endeavour wasn't helped by my hyperactive passengers thumping the windows in a giddy style and making fart noises through the glass. I heard a car horn sound from behind. 'Impatient prick,' I mumbled under my breath – surely they could see my predicament. I managed to slide from my knees and on to my stomach and was now lying face down under my car. To make matters worse it was raining. I could see the pound coin, it was right there under my exhaust in the centre of the car. I reached for it, stretching my hand as far as it could go, forcing me to press my aching abscess cheek down on to the wet tarmac. I made one more grasp with the tips of my fingers to reach for the pound coin (which I swear at one point I could actually hear laughing at me), and then I passed out.

'FLIPPIN ECK!'

(Well, I Was In Earshot Of Four Pre-Schoolers.)

When I woke, I knew immediately where I was: a dentist's surgery. How did I know, you may well ask? Because there was a small transistor radio playing Radio 2 in the corner of the room. Steve Wright in the Afternoon. I believe it's a medical requirement for all dentists to play Radio 2 during surgery.★ That and the fact that I'd passed out with excruciating toothache and was sat in a dentist's chair. That was also a bit of a giveaway.

Apparently I'd been ferried to a twenty-four-hour emergency dentist on the outskirts of Tamworth. And as he bounded into the room looking like a poor man's Adrian Chiles (if that's actually possible), I couldn't help but notice that the dentist was slightly cross-eyed – well, actually more boss-eyed than cross-eyed. You know when somebody seems to be looking just slightly past your eye line when they talk to you, like that doctor in the Cannonball Run films with Burt Reynolds (and if you haven't seen them, shame on you, they're on ITV4 almost every week).

★ Coincidentally (if you'll forgive the pun), Steve actually read that out as a factoid after 'Sunny' by Boney M.

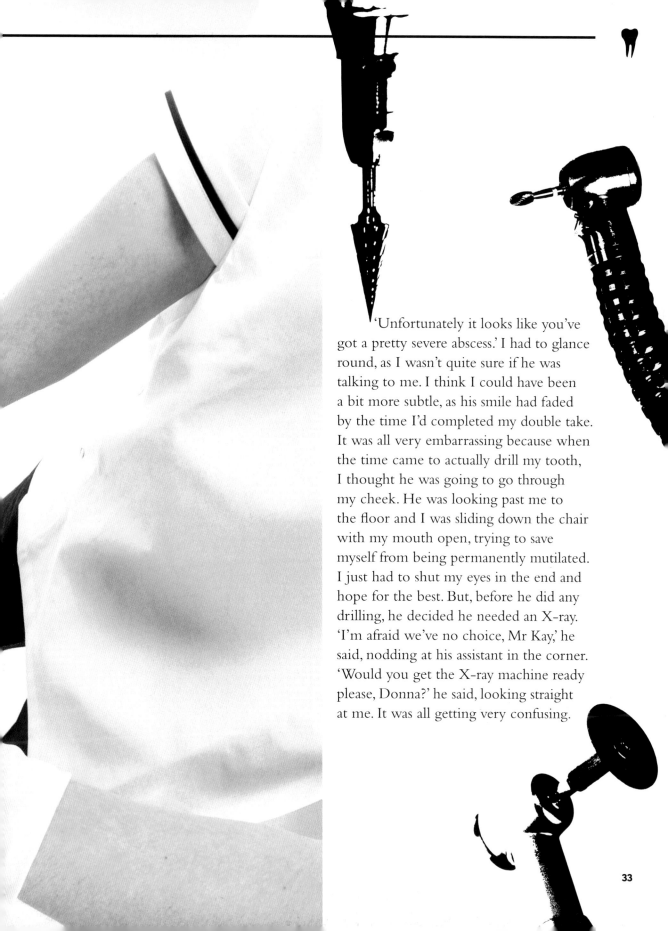

'Unfortunately it looks like you've got a pretty severe abscess.' I had to glance round, as I wasn't quite sure if he was talking to me. I think I could have been a bit more subtle, as his smile had faded by the time I'd completed my double take. It was all very embarrassing because when the time came to actually drill my tooth, I thought he was going to go through my cheek. He was looking past me to the floor and I was sliding down the chair with my mouth open, trying to save myself from being permanently mutilated. I just had to shut my eyes in the end and hope for the best. But, before he did any drilling, he decided he needed an X-ray. 'I'm afraid we've no choice, Mr Kay,' he said, nodding at his assistant in the corner. 'Would you get the X-ray machine ready please, Donna?' he said, looking straight at me. It was all getting very confusing.

33

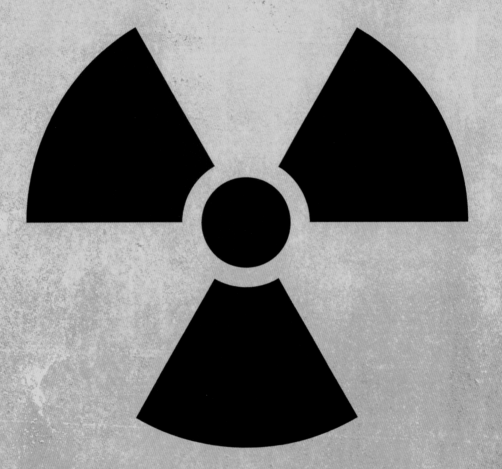

This was the first time I'd ever had to have an X-ray in a dentist's. He lowered a machine down from the ceiling and placed it in front of my face, then I had to bite down on to a piece of plastic. 'Now hold it there,' he said to the window ledge, and both he and Donna started to leg it out of the room. I spat out the plastic, leapt up out of the chair and was off sprinting after them both. I thought the place was on fire.

'No, no, no, you have to stay there, Mr Kay,' he said to the radio. Donna yanked me backwards and into the chair.

'Why?' I said. 'Where are you going?'

'We have to leave the room because of the radiation,' he said, forcing me to bite down on the plastic again.

'RADIATION!' I shouted. Although with the plastic in my mouth it was a bit more like 'ADA-ASHAN!' but it didn't matter as by that time they'd both bolted out of the room.

I thought, Christ! Where are we, Chernobyl? I only came in with an abscess. I'll be driving home with a head like an egg at this rate.

The next thing I knew they had me wearing this pair of protective goggles. They said it was to protect me from any flying debris. I thought, 'I'm right, this is Chernobyl.' Before the dentist started the procedure, he performed one of those mysterious dental check-ups that they do. You know where they talk dentist code as they prod round the inside of your mouth with a spatula. 'Upper right occlusal, lower occlusal five, four, three, two,' he mumbled to Donna, who was taking notes.

Lord knows what it all meant. I had a feeling he was just making it up as he went along.

'... left occlusol ... dogger German bite ... push pineapple shake a tree.'

Then the moment I'd been dreading finally arrived – the injection. My mouth had gone from being brave and wide to a tiny, terrified hole. 'Open wide, Mr Kay,' the dentist ordered in his grey Brummie accent (it was Adrian Chiles). 'Now this may sting a little.' It was actually more of a stab than a sting, the liar. I mean, why don't they just tell the truth? Surely it'd be better for everyone in the long run? My knuckles whitened as my fingernails dug in through my jeans and ripped into the flesh on my legs. Fortunately I was distracted from this agony by having a four-inch needle impaled directly into the centre of my abscess.

The next thing I knew Donna was sucking … Hey, grow up! I didn't go private. She had that metal tube thing in my mouth and was extracting the excess blood, and believe me there was plenty of it, with Dr Adrian Crippen Chiles drilling away at my molars.

He started with that really deep drill that has so much bass that it shakes through your entire body. I hate the noise it makes; it sounded like I had a biker from Junior Kick Start scrambling around the inside of my mouth.

Then as he briefly removed the drill I took the liberty of performing a quick inspection of his work so far by flicking my tongue around the infected area. The only problem with this, as you might have noticed, is that your tongue has a bad habit of magnifying things.

'OH MY GOD!'
I thought.
'HOW BIG IS THIS HOLE HE'S DRILLED?'

I was only having a routine abscess treated and this lunatic was clearly erecting a shopping centre in the inside of my mouth. I half expected to look in the mirror and see two blokes in hard hats stood on the edge of my gums inspecting plans as the other reversed a lorry carrying a skip over my teeth. This man was clearly a psychopath.

I realised I didn't even know where I was. My last memory was seeing the Fat Controller having a crafty fag and that cheeky pound coin hiding under my car. Suddenly I felt like Dustin Hoffman in Marathon Man, but before I had a chance to voice my concern he was straight back in with another drill.

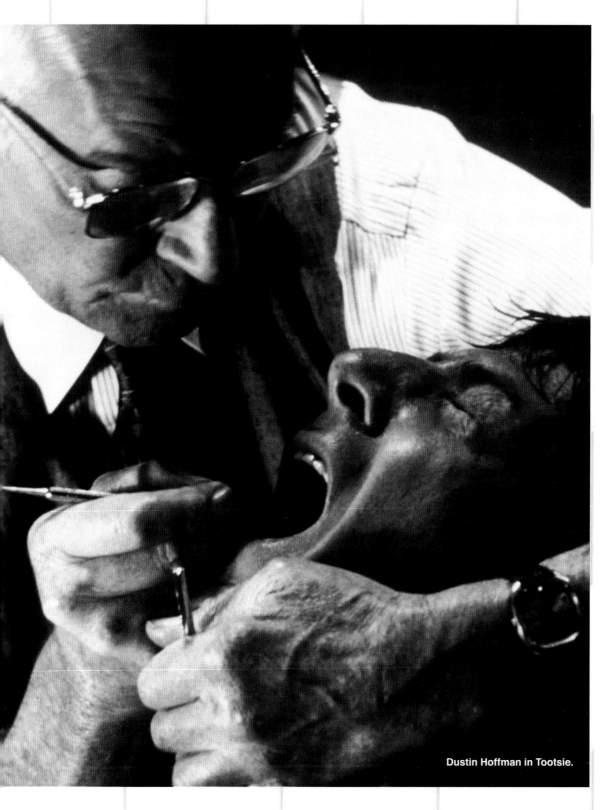

Dustin Hoffman in Tootsie.

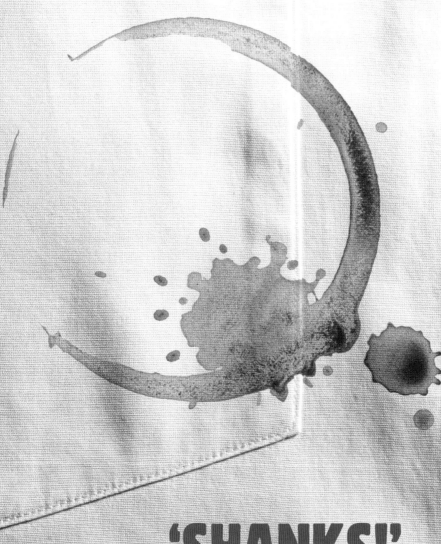

'GET A COASHTER, GET A COASHTER,'

'SHANKS!'

This time it was the obligatory high-pitched piercing drill that had me joining in with some involuntary high-pitched squeals of my own. I bet the dogs around the surgery were having a field day, cocking their heads to one side at the sound of the horror that lay within. Then, to add insult to injury, the cheeky pig started to use my chest as a workbench. He lay his drill on there, then a scalpel. I had to draw the line when he put his brew down. 'Get a coashter, get a coashter,' I slurred at him. 'I don't want a cup ring on my best shirt.'

Then, after what felt like fourteen hours (it was actually just under ten minutes), he finished. I thanked him 'Shanks!' (Shanks for what I'll never know, but manners cost nothing and I wasn't dragged up, unlike him putting his brew down without a coashter.) And then Donna invited me to have a rinse. I nodded politely, swilled it around my mouth – numb from the anaesthetic – and spat it straight down the front of my best shirt.

Bewildered, I staggered out to greet the receptionist.

'Are you free in six months' time on a Tuesday at a quarter past four?' she asked me.

How the hell was I supposed to know that? 'I haven't got a clue, love, I can't even see colours right now.'

'That's three hundred and forty-three pounds,' she said.

'I heard that. I've no problem understanding that. Three hundred and forty-three pounds? You should be

wearing a mask and a striped jumper you robbing—' but I didn't finish off my sentence as I was distracted by the amount of spit I was gobbing on both the counter and the receptionist. She then handed me one of those credit card machines while discreetly wiping my spit off the counter top with her cardigan sleeve. If I hadn't been so disorientated from the anaesthetic, I'd've laughed at the way she turned her head in an effort to give both me and my secret PIN number some privacy.

They always do that in restaurants when the time comes for you to pay the bill. The waiter hands you the machine and then deliberately turns away, probably to a mirror on the ceiling that reflects you typing your PIN number. It could be worse, my nana has PIN number Tourette's. She gets to the checkout in Sainsbury's and as she types it in she shouts it out for all to hear, 'Six-four-seven-three.' While all the local smackheads type it into their mobiles and then follow her and her tartan Sholley home.

After going through all that, the dentist said he could only do so much and ended up referring me to a Russian doctor down at the hospital. There followed another bloody X-ray, by which time I was starting to feel like a Japanese fisherman I'd had that much radiation. Scrutinising my scans, the doctor called me over and said, 'You see this grey area here, under your tooth?'

I nodded obligingly.

'Well, that is all buggered.' Come again, I thought to myself, 'buggered'? Is that an official medical term? I've never heard Charlie say that on Casualty.

'Unfortunately your bottom tooth is the same; your root has collapsed and this has all gone pear-shaped.'

Pear-shaped? Now he was blatantly blinding me with his medical jargon.

As my bottom tooth had gone pear-shaped and the other one was buggered, he recommended tooth implants and booked me in for a simple procedure that he assured me would be 'a piece of piss'. I'm lying – he didn't say that.

I turned up at the hospital with my dressing gown, slippers and rosary beads in a Next carrier bag (good carrier bags, Next). Finally the anaesthetist rolled in, and after asking me when I'd last eaten (fajitas the previous tea time) and if I was allergic to anything (I told him straight – cats and face paints), he then casually asked me if I would mind posing for a photo with him and whipped out his camera phone. I had to say no. I mean, there's a time and a place and I had one of those gowns on with my arse out and was shitting bangers over my 'minor' tooth op. The last thing I needed was for that image to be sprawled across t'internet. Then common sense prevailed, and I relented – you don't want to fall out with the anaesthetist before an operation, you might never wake up.

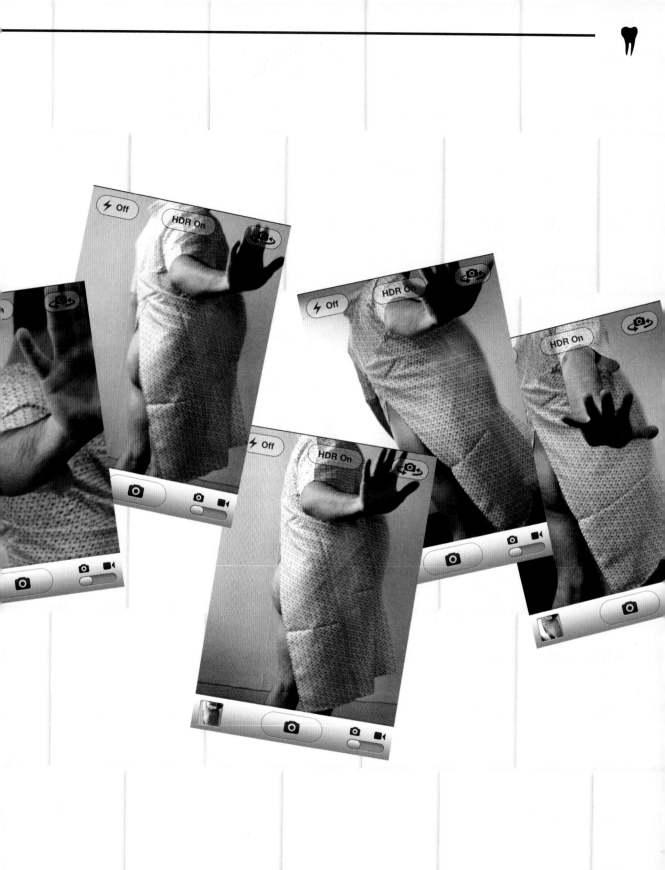

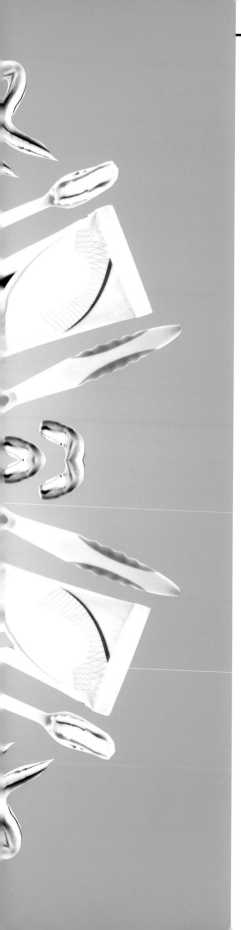

I was on pins by the time I saw him again in theatre. I expected him to be waiting with a full camera crew and a boom mic. He went to inject the back of my hand. 'You're about to feel a little scratch,' he said. Another lying bastard – it wasn't a scratch, it was more of a sharp, agonising tear of flesh. 'Arsehole,' I winced to myself. I nodded at the doors in the operating theatre and said, 'What's through there, a photographic studio?' I had visions of photos turning up of me heavily sedated with my head poking through comedy holes like those things you see at a fairground. I was out for the count. Well, not exactly out, I was sedated, and can recall the Russian surgeon occasionally asking me to open wide and him cracking open a bottle of beer on my teeth. I also recall asking everybody in the room if they would high-five each other, and at the end of the procedure I took great delight in announcing that I had in fact come in for a vasectomy. Rule one: if you know you're under sedation, try and keep your mouth shut.

When I came round I was in agony, and I mean agony. The nurse said, 'I'll give you some painkillers,' and gave me some Paracetamol. I thought you said 'painkillers'! I can get these from the pound shop down the road. When a nurse says painkillers, I want morphine. I am a bloke after all. This is why blokes could never have babies and if they did they'd only ever have one because they'd still be in a state of shock over the pain.

They sent me away with a denture to wear but I couldn't speak with it in. I sounded just like Louie Spence. They also told me to go and visit the dental hygienist. Another waste of time, as basically all they do is just bollock you for not brushing your teeth and make you feel as though you have a mouth like Shane MacGowan out of The Pogues. It reminds me a bit of going to confession as a kid, where I'd lie and

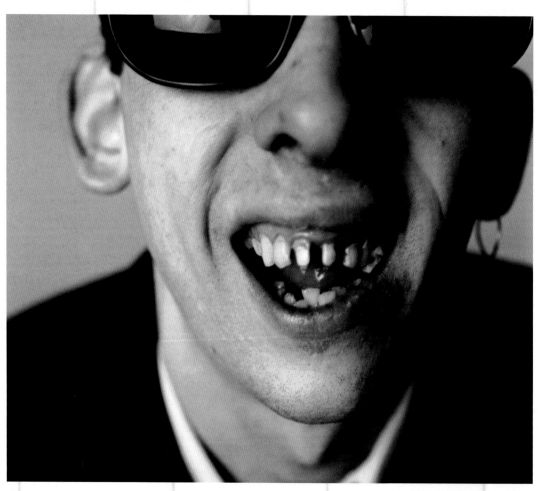

promise not to do it again knowing damn well I would.

'I promise you I'll floss every day. In fact I'll go straight to the chemist when I leave here and buy some.★ The next time you see me I'll have a smile like Donny Osmond (or even better, Shaun Ryder).' Anyway, against my better judgement I went to see the hygienist. A waste of even more money – thirty quid to have a scale and polish with an orbital sander; thirty quid to get sprayed in my own blood. I came out looking like Carrie when she goes to the prom.

★ ... and a whistle lolly, because for some reason chemists always sell them.

People are obsessed with having white teeth these days and they'll stop at nothing to get them. They'll even wear a gumshield filled with acid to bed every night – talk about a passion killer. I notice that people have become more obsessed with personal hygiene too, washing every day, which puts me to shame when I think about it because when I was growing up I used to have one bath a week, every Sunday night with Mr Matey. He was a widower, lived four doors down, quiet man, always had the tap end.

And if you wanted a hot bath in our house you had to plan ahead and put the immersion on the previous Wednesday. Even then it would still only be lukewarm.★ My mum would still have to come up with the kettle full of hot water and top up the bath. 'Move down!' she'd shout. 'Move down, it's boiling hot, it'll burn you,' and sure enough it'd do just that, bouncing off the sides of the bath and on to my naked flesh. I've got a back like the Singing Detective in a certain light.

Today's generation doesn't know what cold is, with their fancy combi boilers and central heating. I used to have steam coming off my breath when I got up in the morning it was that cold. And apart from a severe case of near-fatal pneumonia, which cost me the hearing in my left ear, it never did me any harm. If we wanted heat we had to make do with a coat thrown over the bed, or my dad installing his economy DIY heating scheme that he saw on Magpie and involved him stretching some kind of industrial clingfilm over every bedroom window in the house and then blowing it with a hairdryer. It was still freezing.

★ **Sorry … I've forgotten. It was nothing.**

My mum did her bit by making her own draught excluders – you remember those huge snake draught excluders that used to lie behind the doors. Not only were they successful in keeping in the heat, if you can call it that, they also came in very handy whenever R Julie and me had a fight. Once she used one to garrotte me after she discovered I'd recorded over her copy of 'Marillion Live in Concert' with an episode of Boon. I got my revenge by pouring cold water down her back when she was in the bath with me. We always used to bath together – and no, I'm not getting all Flowers in the Attic on you. That's just what you did in those days to save on the heating bills. In fact we only stopped because she got a full-time job working at Sainsbury's and left home (I'm joking! Jesus!! It was M&S).

Finally having the bath to myself meant I could spread out a bit and bring in almost all of my toys. I'd have a whale

of a time playing. One my favourite games was 'storm at sea', where I'd place Chewbacca and Stretch Armstrong★ on a makeshift Lego raft in the middle of the bath and then watch them slowly sink under a torrential downpour which I'd create with the colander out of the kitchen.

My mum would bring up the Fairy Liquid so I could make some bubbles. Although I vividly remember the time she once used Persil and I went to Cubs with a rash on my privates. Then, when I was wrinkled enough, my mum would wash my hair in either Vosene or Timotei and rinse off the water with a large measuring jug. I always wondered why they didn't show that on the advert. Then again I suppose seeing a middle-aged woman on her knees tipping grey bathwater over her son with a measuring jug may not have been considered good marketing in the 1970s.

★ Size and scale means nothing to a child.

Things were much more glamorous back then. Take the Imperial Leather family, for example. They certainly gave me something to aspire to on that advert. Talk about a life of luxury – they were so rich they would travel by train whilst sitting in a bath, each! They even had their own Imperial Leather soap delivered to them en route.

Thanks to that advert, Imperial Leather was considered a sign of success when I was growing up. Now you can get three bars for a pound from Mr Thrifty on the main road. In our house we usually had two choices of soap: Lifebuoy or boring old Shield. Though I have to admit my mum would crack open a bar of Imperial Leather over the festive period, even if it was just to keep up with the Joneses. It always made me laugh because by New Year's Eve all that was left was the Imperial Leather sticker on a tiny square of soap.

People are much more body-conscious now, especially men. Today it's all metrosexuality. Men like to take an interest in their appearance, and even go so far as swapping stag dos for pamper days. Treating themselves to manicures, pedicures, Botox, balls waxed (everybody talk about … mmm, pop music), it's a completely different generation. Most of the blokes I know in their sixties and seventies won't even wear deodorant – they consider it to be the work of the devil. My uncle Nobhead never wears deodorant – he thinks it'll rob him of his masculinity. He can't see the point and usually rants, 'What's wrong with smelling like a man?'

I say, 'Men aren't supposed to smell like tramp's arseholes. Get into the twenty-first century.'

What makes me laugh is that he works on security at the airport, checking bags and frisking people. He's got access to more deodorant than Superdrug. He's confiscating cases of the stuff on a daily basis; you'd think he might just open some and use it.

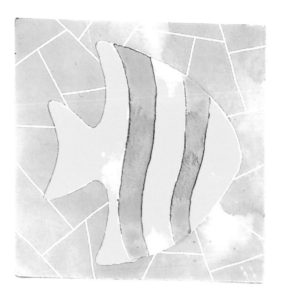

I've always thought that's been a bloody scam since 9/11. Do you think that's what the late Osama Bin Laden had in mind? Forcing us to pay £2 for a clear polythene bag? They even have a vending machine that sells them at the airport. Just so you can put your toiletries in it and make sure you've nothing over 100 ml. Why not? Who's going to bring a plane down with a can of Lynx Africa?

Ironically, while my uncle Nobhead refuses to freshen up his armpits, he is concerned about his appearance and still uses a sunbed. He goes to Tantastic (over the dry cleaner's) every Wednesday, pensioner's Wednesday. He swears by them. 'I've been using sunbeds for years and there's nothing wrong with them and there's nothing wrong with me,' he's always saying, while his hair's coming out in clumps. He's like a tanned Gollum with BO.

Osama. April 2003, Dave's Stag Newquay

Sunbeds used to be very popular at one time – everybody used them. You couldn't walk down the street at night without seeing a bedroom window lit up with electric neon blue. We hired one once, £25 for a week. Small bloke with a beard brought it round in the back of a Citroën. It wasn't even a full sunbed, it was just the top half which we had to erect above the bed. Everybody wanted to use it. We couldn't move for family and friends wanting to kick-start their tans for the summer. It should have cost us a fortune in electricity, but luckily my dad had the foresight to wire it up to the lamppost in the back street.

Time marches on and sunbeds are now widely considered to be death traps. People have moved on to false tans now, in an effort to have a bit of colour without the health hazards. My uncle Nobhead hates them.

'You know why they're called false tans? It's because they look false. If you want to waltz around stinking of curry and looking like an Oompa Loompa with a bright orange face, be my guest – I'm sticking with the sunbed.'

Gene Wilder in Stir Crazy

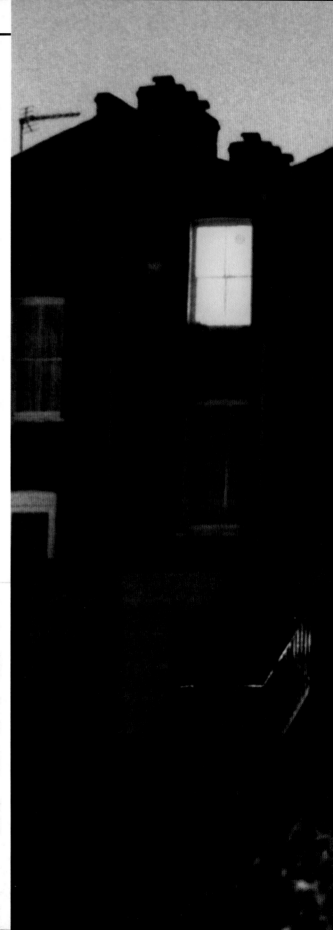

I think people have become way too cautious when it comes to sunlight – they've gone to the other extreme now. I know some parents who won't even let their children so much as look through the window without a pair of sunglasses, let alone take a step outside on a sunny day unless they're caked in Factor 40 sunscreen.

'Where are you going? Get back here!' Then they drag their pale and blinking children back inside and smother cream all over them.

'Now go and have some fun,' they say, pushing them out the door, their faces all white. **'AAAH**

HH!! IT'S IN MY EYES ...
IT'S IN MY EYES,
I CAN'T SEE!'

'DON'T YOU DARE
WIPE IT OFF! YOU'LL BURN
IF YOU DO!!'

But at the end of the day it doesn't seem to matter whether it's fake or real, people love to have a tan as it signifies a healthy and happy lifestyle.

I envy the people who tan easily. You bump into them in the street and say, 'Oh you're brown, have you been away?'

'No, have I heck,' they reply with pride. 'Back garden at the weekend this, that's only place I've been.'

My dad loved having a tan and if it was a sunny day he'd leg it home from work as quick as he could, strip off, drag an emergency chair into the back yard and bathe in the warmth of the evening sun until it set behind the launderette across the road. He wouldn't dream of using anything like sunscreen. 'Deirdre, pass me some cooking oil,' he'd shout over his shoulder into the kitchen. 'Crisp and Dry.' Then later he'd go out playing snooker with my uncle Nobhead smelling like a big chip. People didn't want sun protection in the 1980s, they wanted to burn. That was the whole point 'BURN ME!!' and bollocks to the consequences.

My dad loved the sun and hated the rain, which always made me wonder why we went to Butlins every year for our holidays, where it would piss it down every day for a fortnight. I remember actually seeing him cry in Pwllheli, he was that angry with the weather.

'Come on sun,' he'd snarl through gritted teeth as he pulled back the curtains each morning. 'Where are you?'

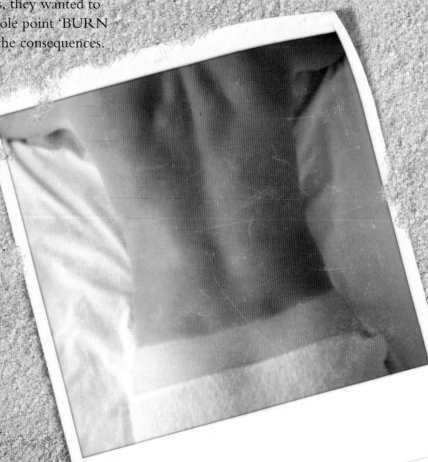

The only other times I saw my dad cry was when the IRA★ kidnapped Shergar and when he trapped his balls in a sun lounger in Lloret de Mar. I'll never forget it. It was one of those cheap and nasty white plastic sun loungers with an almost invisible hairline crack running right up the centre of one of its slats. It lay by the side of the pool, patiently waiting for some unsuspecting fool to sit down, and then along came my dad.

Fresh from a dip in the pool, he leapt from the water like a gazelle and strode vigorously towards the sun lounger that my uncle Nobhead had strategically commandeered with a beach towel at half-past four that very morning. (Needs must on the Costa Brava.) And then, without so much as blinking, he sat down. Completely unbeknownst to him his weight shifting to the back of the sun lounger allowed the crack in the plastic slat to open its jaws just wide enough to let his family jewels plop through the gap and into its mouth. They were already hanging low from being under water for twenty minutes so they needed little, if any, encouragement. It was like sitting on a mantrap and as I sailed past on my Lilo I couldn't help but laugh. Regretfully I said nothing, a regret I carry to this day, as what happened next still makes me shudder and wince.

With his head slowly cooking in the midday sun, my dad searched for protection. 'Deirdre? Deirdre, have you seen my sun hat?' Then he spotted it, just out of arm's reach next to yesterday's *Daily Mirror*. 'Deirdre, will you pass me my—' And then unsuspectingly he leaned forward, causing the widened crack on the plastic slat to snap shut on his genitalia.

' ... HAAAA

AAAAAAAAHGGGG - T!!'

It took five of us to lift him into the back of the ambulance; he was still sat on the sun lounger. Completely delirious from the pain, he was, I remember him begging my mum to quickly go and 'pick my dick up before it rolls into the pool'. He spent the rest of the fortnight kicking his balls down the beach … Well at least they got a tan.

My dad also used to hate wasting sunshine. If it was the big summer holidays and I was off school, he'd sometimes catch me in the front room watching telly, and if it was a sunny day he'd lose his mind.

'What are you doing?'

'I'm watching The Karate Kid.'

'Well bugger the bloody Karate Kid and get outside. Have you seen the weather out there?' he'd say, ripping open the curtains that I'd previously closed to keep the sun out of my eyes. 'They'll think someone's died over the road … Look at the sunshine, it's glorious, now get outside and enjoy it,' he'd order me whilst flicking off the TV. 'Don't waste this, it could be raining tomorrow.'

And then when it did rain he'd make us all stand at the front room window and watch. You know when you get those big storms in summer, when the sky goes purple and grey in about two

minutes and people go round saying stupid things like, 'Oh, we need this, we're ready for this … just what we need to clear things out, dust things down.' Just because we've had three or four days of beautiful, uninterrupted sunny weather, the miserable swines. When those electrical storms came, it was only a matter of minutes before the heavens would open and the rains would come flooding down. That's when my dad would gather us all at the front room window.

'HEY! R JULIE, PETER, DEIRDRE, QUICK! COME AND LOOK AT THIS RAIN, IT'S BIBLICAL!!'

and we'd grudgingly stand and watch the rain as it hit the ground.

'Look at that! Bloody hell, it's bouncing it down now,' he'd say with an excited laugh. 'Hey, look at Kathleen's gutters over the road … She'll have to get them fixed,' and then he'd wave at her through the window and point to her roof, mee-mawing her problem as if she could actually see him.

'KATHLEEN, LOVE, YOUR DOWNSPOUT, IT'S PISSING OUT!'

gesturing rainfall with his hands.

Then, sure enough, the thunder and lightning would arrive and my mum would lose her mind,

'SACRED HEART OF GOD! QUICK THE TELEVISION!'

she'd shout whilst leaping over into the corner, reaching behind the telly and ripping out the aerial. I've still not seen the end of The Karate Kid – does he win?

'WE DON'T WANT THE HOUSE TO BLOW UP!'

'What? When have you ever known somebody's house to blow up?'

But she was having none of it. She's always been a worrier, my mum. Every Sunday night after London's Burning she used to go round the house, unplugging everything, just in case it spontaneously caught fire.

She's still the same today. We had one of those big late summer storms a few weeks ago and she called me up in the middle of it.

'Have you got this storm yet?'

'Not yet.'

'Well you will have it in five minutes, it's on its way across town to you now. I'm sitting here in darkness. Quick, you'd better get off the phone before it blows up.'

'Mum, the phone won't blow up bec— Mum? MUM??' But she'd already hung up.

But that's the British weather and there's nothing you can do about it, except move. My nan makes me laugh, she said: 'It's ridiculous, they wanna do something about this.'

I said, 'Who's they?'

'The bloody government, it's a disgrace. I've never known rain like it.'

I thought, you're eighty-nine years old, surely you must have known rain like it.

My nana's fantastic though. She's still very happy in her warden-controlled flat on the other side of town, with her red rope hanging from the ceiling in case there's ever an emergency.

She's only ever pulled it once when she had a wasp in her front room.

The warden came on over the speaker. 'Is everything all right, Mrs Kay?'

'No, I've got a wasp flying round here. He's been in here all day and he's a big bugger, he's like a zeppelin.'

How she knew it was male, I'll never know; it's not as though the wasp was flying around sporting a cock and balls. If that stung you, you'd know about it – it could take your eye out.

'Unless it's a health and safety risk, Mrs Kay, my hands are tied… Have you tried a rolled-up TV guide or a slipper?'

Pulling the emergency cord for the warden over a wasp wasn't a surprise to me. That's what old people do, they blow things out of all proportion.

Like the time my nana's kitchen tap wouldn't stop dripping. I'm amazed you haven't heard about it already, because you'd have thought it had been reported on CNN the way my nana was going on about it.

'It's still dripping,' she said as I answered my mobile. Not even a 'hello' or a 'how are you?'.

'Did you call the plumber?' I said.

'Yes I did and he sent that young lad round who works with him.'

'And did he do anything?'

'He put a washer on it and tightened it up.'

'And did you pay him?'

'He said he didn't want any money but I gave him a fiver.'

'A FIVER!!'

'Yes, I said "Here, have this and split it with your mate outside in the van."'

'Two pounds fifty? Each? No wonder your tap's still dripping – a bloody washer costs more than that!'

But no matter what you tell her, she'll still do what she wants. I turned up at her flat the other week and she was nowhere to be seen. Then I heard a buzzing noise coming from outside.

I OPENED THE WINDOW TO FIND MY NAN STOOD ON A STEPLADDER STRIMMING HER BUSH.

'Nan! What are you doing?' I shouted through the window.

'IT NEEDED DOING, IT WAS DRIVING ME MAD.'

I went outside and took the hedge strimmer from her to finish off her pruning.

'Wait! Wait!' she said. 'Let me hold the ladder.'

I said, 'That's rich, who was holding it for you?'

I do worry about my nan managing on her own and, last year, after much resistance, she finally let me organise a home help for her. So now she has a lady who comes round to help her out, you know, doing some bits around her flat. My nan was a bit frosty with her at first. Then things slowly started to thaw and they got talking and my nan discovered that she wasn't British,

'You've got a bit of an accent, haven't you – where are you from?'

'Originally I come from Germany.'

'Germany, oh really?' she said, delighted. 'Well I used to make ammunition for Lancashire bombers, love. Stick the kettle on, we're practically family.'

The poor lady looked shell-shocked, not unlike her own family.

Sadly my nan fell and broke her wrist last winter. She slipped on some leaves outside Farm Foods. But, typical of her generation, she just got back up on her feet, picked up her two bags of shopping, walked over to the bus station where she then caught her bus and then walked all the way up the hill back to her flat before she rang me. She's as tough as old boots and there's me lying on the bedroom floor screaming I'm Christopher Reeve because I've tripped over one of my wife's shoes.

'Peter, I think I've broken my wrist.'

She thinks? Her thumb was on the wrong way round.

'Right, I'm on my way over now. Put some ice on it, have you got any ice?'

And then I could hear her banging around in the freezer, searching for ice.

'No, I've not got any ice, Peter.'

'Well, can you not put something else on it? Have you got any frozen peas?'

Then the phone went quiet again while she fumbled around in her kitchen.

'I've got tinned … I've got tinned peas, are they any good?'

God love her.

'NO, YOU CAN'T PUT TINNED PEAS ON A BROKEN WRIST, NANA.'

PLEASE COULD YOU STOP MY PAPERS!

The residents are always falling over in her flats. She said, 'Hey, did I tell you about Lena over the way [pointing] falling over and breaking her hip?'

'No.'

'Well Lena's fallen over and broken her hip.'

'I know, you just told me,' I said, confused.

'She fell over, Saturday afternoon it was, right in the middle of Monk. She got up to get the remote – she keeps it by the side of the telly – and she went over. Th'ambulance men came and they didn't have a key so they had to kick her back doors in. She was shook up and when they were taking her down the stairs on a stretcher and she saw me she leaned over and said, 'Mrs Kay, will you stop my papers?'

That's exactly what I mean about old people blowing everything out of proportion. Talk about getting your priorities right. Poor Lena's being carted off to the hospital and the only thing she can think about in a time of crisis is getting her newspapers stopped. Mind you, I can see her point. She eventually gets out of hospital after two or three months with MRSA or whatever other superbug they've got going this week and then when she finally makes it back home she can't open her front door for all the bloody newspapers that are wedged behind it. It's one disaster after another. She'll probably end up breaking her other hip trying to bash the front door open and then we're back to square one.

My nan said,

'THE DOCTOR'S GOT HER ON PEN-EE-SALIN,'

and that's not my bad spelling, that's exactly how she pronounced it. She's forever getting her words wrong, like the time she asked me if I'd seen 'that film that won all the Oscars with those big tall blue men – Abattoir', or when she told me to slow down in the car because my driving was too 'erotic'. I was laughing that much I almost mounted the kerb and hit an Indian lady.

I took her to McDonald's the other week and, looking up at the menu above the counter, I asked what she wanted. Bewildered, she paused and, after studying the menu closely for some time she said, 'I'll think I'll try one of those wiffy', and pointed to a sign above the counter that said 'free Wi-fi'. 'In fact, if they're free I think I'll have two.'

And recently she told me how much she enjoyed watching Saturday Kitchen and asked if the next time I was in the Co-op I could pick up 'some of that orgasmic veg'. I didn't know where to look.

th'iPod nana

'PETER, CAN YOU GET ON THAT FACETUBE AND TALK TO YOUR FRIENDS?'

She's quite technically minded for her age. I got her an iPod for Mother's Day – or should I say 'th'iPod', because that's what she calls it. 'Peter where's th'iPod?' It's usually down the side of the couch with the remote for her VD player.

When I first gave it to her she thought it was a blank cassette. She was trying to put it into her tape player. 'It won't fit, Peter, it won't fit this.'

'It's an iPod, Nana, there's over a thousand of your favourite songs on this thing.'

She gave a look of incomprehension I'll never forget, from me, to the iPod and back again. As if to say, 'What? A thousand songs? On this thing?'

'Yes, I've put them all on here for you: Ol' Blue Eyes, Frank Sinatra, Seal.'

God love her but she still can't work it. I just sit it in the docking station, turn it on and leave it playing all week. She has it on shuffle 24/7 and turns the volume up and down when she wants to hear it. She still can't comprehend that you can get all of those songs on to something so small (and if I'm completely honest with you, neither can I).

I find the speed at which technology is moving completely overwhelming.
Oh, I understand how iPods work – songs get converted into MP3 files (he says, scratching his head), but it only seems like a few months ago when I thought I was the dog's bollocks because I was driving around with a five-disc multichangeable CD player in the boot of my car. They were great until I had to change a disc, and then I'd find myself stood on the hard shoulder in the rain, with my hazard lights on, trying to shove Gabrielle into my boot, the fine rain pouring down my CD cartridge so my discs wouldn't play.

That's another thing that's always wound me up, almost as much as coat hangers and Go Compare, the inadequacy of CDs. I remember when they first came out, everybody was going mad for them. 'CDs are fantastic! They're indestructible. You can spread jam on one, throw it across a car park and it'll still play.' What a load of horseshit. If you get just a single drop of water on a CD it's knackered. Get a spot of grease on one and suddenly you're Fatboy Slim and it's skipping all over the place. And I've never yet met anybody who was stupid enough to spread jam on their £40 copy of Brothers in Arms, let alone throw it across a car park.

DAVID GREY –
WHITE LADDER

DIGITAL
RECORDING
2
3302 025
STEREO

Adamski – Musical Pharmacy

STEREO

All rights reserved. Copying, public performance and broad-
csting prohibited.

ENIGMA – MCMXC DISC ONE

5 – 2055
STEREO

A

RECORDING PRODUCED BY   c.55

Maxi Priest – Bonafide

℗ 1987

Lato 1
TGNK
79

LP 69-999
© Not Just A Record – Record

Side 1
33⅓ RPM
Stereo

mum's Favourite Songs –

C90
stereo

A
SIDE

(Dina Carroll one on this side)

T'PAU – BRIDGE OF SPIES.

ML-A02

A
SIAE
MADE
IN ITALY

TUTTI I DIRITTI DEL PRODUTTORE FONOGRAFICO S DEL
PROPRIETARIO DELLE OPERE RIPRODOTTE SONO RISER-
VATI. DUPLICAZIONE, ESECUZIONE PUBBLICA E RADIODIF-
FUSIONE DI QUESTO NASTRO MAGNETICO SONO PROIBITI.

25 B
MARTIKA'S KITCHEN

STEREO

A Then Jericho – ORCHESTRA
Big Area.

LN
C-60

MUM'S TAPE. DO NOT USE.
~~THORNBIRDS~~ HOLBY CITY
~~GHOSTWATCH~~

CDs are becoming a thing of the past and the days of having just five discs in the boot of my car seem archaic. Now I've got th'iPod in my glove compartment and I've gone from one extreme to the other, with access to over fifteen thousand songs at the touch of a button. And yet despite that I STILL can't find anything decent to listen to. I drive my family mad on car journeys.

'What's this? Crap. Next.' Play another song 'What's this one? Crap. Next,' and I try another song. I honestly believe my children have never heard a song the whole way through. I'm sure they think all songs only last twenty seconds.

I find it strange to think that they'll never experience things like records and cassette tapes. I was going through my LPs the other day and I was laughing because my children thought they were big black CDs. I'd already spent half an hour trying to explain the concept of videotapes to them. Even I was shocked at how big videotapes look now. I've still got hundreds of them, and records, and cassette tapes, I just can't let myself throw any of them out. My wife goes mad, 'When are you going to get rid of all this shit?'

'SHIT? SHIT YOU SAY? THAT'S LIKE A KNIFE IN MY HEART!'

Mind you, one man's shit is another man's gold, and if you ever need proof of that just spend ten minutes on eBay, because you can get rid of any old shit on there and get paid for it.

SWAPSHOP · TOYAH WILCOX · MY Web Browser   Sign In

Categories   Groovy stuff   Special Offers
⟲ Back to homepage › Pop Stars › Photographs › Toyah Wilcox

Toyah Wilcox signed photo
Condition: Excellent

£0.34   BUY NOW
                         Watch this item

Postage: £1.50 Standard delivery – see details
Delivery time: 2-3 working days
Payments: Postal Orders only – see details
Returns: No returns accepted

⬤ swapshop Buyer Protection
              Learn More

Item Description   Postage/delivery

Very much sought after signed picture of Toyah Wilcox which
she kindly signed for me at Thames Studios fresh from filming
Give Us a Clue, circ 1986.
Reason for sale: transgender op fund

If someone would have told me ten years ago that a car-boot sale on t'internet would be a multi-billion worldwide success, I'd have thought they were on glue. I love the complete randomness of it all. I mean, you can literally get absolutely anything and in no time at all. I wanted five yards of denim, a set of radiator valves and a signed picture of Toyah. I got the lot in less than five minutes.

My wife suggested I try selling my videos on there, but I could never part with them. And besides, even technology has moved on again. DVDs are already becoming a thing of the past. Now people want Blu-ray. Blue Ray was a bloke near me. He had a look of Wolf from Gladiators and sold pornos out of the boot of a Nissan Sunny round the back of our local park. 'Bit of blue Ray for the dads', that was his catchphrase. I was watching The Gadget Show the other week and when I heard them said 'Blu-ray's big in Asia', I nearly choked on my Arctic Roll.

I thought, 'Christ, he's done well for himself.'

People say, 'Oh you've got to watch it on Blu-ray, the quality is amazing.'

But I begrudge buying Blu-ray. Take, for example, the Star Wars films. I've got them on video, I've got them on DVD – if they get any clearer I'll expect to be sat on the couch in the front room with Yoda having a brew. And if it ends up in 3D, I can help him dip his HobNobs.

But as much as people are embracing future technology, they also can't seem to shake off their old habits. I still find myself saying, 'There's nothing on telly tonight, do you fancy going to the video shop for a DVD?' Because, as far back as I can remember, it's always been referred to as the video shop. So we get a take-out and call in at the video shop. Some things never change; we attempt to pick a film but just end up picking a fight with each other because me and my wife can never find anything we agree on. I want an action film and she usually wants a rom-com or one of those true stories that'll break your heart about an orphan boy with no arms and legs who makes it to the Olympics. We end up getting both films and after queuing for what feels like an eternity, with our now lukewarm Chinese, the shop assistant tells us that because we've got two films we're now entitled to a third one, free. So off we go again.

Then it's back home for a cold Chinese and we're both fast asleep on the couch, before the little boy has even reached the orphanage, let alone the Olympics. These days I've usually nodded off before the trailers have ended, or at least by the time that god-awful advert that warns you about the dangers of video piracy comes on. You know the one that they won't let you fast-forward through, the one with that annoyingly loud dance music where the voiceover guy says, 'You wouldn't steal a car.'

Well no, I wouldn't steal a car, but trust me there's a big difference between

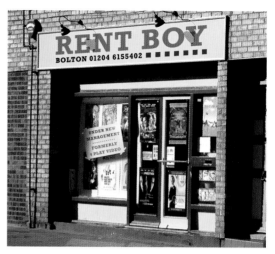

stealing a car and watching a knock-off version of Abattoir.

Then, like a tight arse, I try to watch all the DVDs on Sunday afternoon so I can get my money's worth before they have to be back to the shop for seven. I could open a video shop on the amount of late fines I've had to pay over the years. In fact I'm still banned from Bolton Video Centre for forgetting to take Jumanji back for four weeks. I could have sworn I had, but then I found the disc down the side of the couch along with two pounds in loose change and a dog-eared copy of the Koran.

Anyway, because almost all the video shops in Bolton have now closed down and because I'm banned from the remaining ones, we've had to resort to the new way of hiring DVDs, and that's through one of those websites where you supposedly pick your top ten favourites and they send them to you in the post. The problem is I can't ever find the discs to send back and I always do have to send them back because they've usually sent me the wrong DVD.

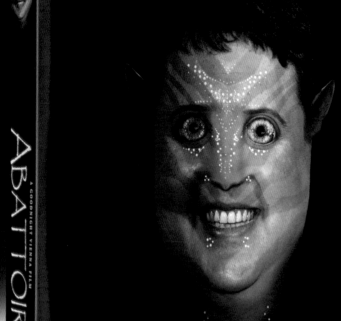

YOU'LL HONESTLY SHIT YOUR PANTS

A GOODNIGHT VIENNA FILM

ABATTOIR

18

We're addicted to boxed sets now. You know, those boxed sets of series – we can't get enough of them. We can't stop watching them, especially the American ones. We'll do six or seven episodes a night. They're better than films because they're shorter and snappier and they get you hooked, so that when one is finished my wife will say, 'Go on, stick another one on.'

'But it's half one in the morning and I've got be up early.'

I'm like 'NO! This is getting beyond a joke. It's a quarter to four now and I'm sitting here in my own piss and shit, with matchsticks in my eyes.'

'PUT DISC FOUR IN NOW!'

So I go to get disc four but the stupid arseholes at the online DVD company have sent us the bloody 'bonus features' disc instead. So now we have to wait another three weeks before disc four finally arrives in the post, by which time the momentum has vanished and we can't remember where we were in the story and then the disc won't play because there's a spot of jam on it.

If you want to watch a full series, the best thing you can do is get one of those recordable hard drive thingy-ma-jigs. Now they are the dog's bollocks. No more fannying around at the video shop and no more wrong discs in the post. Just one push of a button and you can have the lot. And all you've got to do on Sky Plus is push the green button for series link and it's job done, piece of piss. In fact I think Sky should use that last line for one of their marketing campaigns. 'Sky – Job done, piece of piss.' If you ever see that on a billboard you'll know where it's come from.

'Go on, stick another one on – I've got to see what happens.' She's like a junkie.

So we watch another one and we're left with another 'to be continued' hook.

'Oh please! Just stick one more on.'

I have to be honest with you, Sky Plus is right up there with sunlight and running water as far as necessities go in my life. If someone turns up at the front door and says, 'Mr Kay, I'm afraid we're digging up the top of the road and your gas is going to be cut off for a few hours', I have to admit I'm annoyed. But if somebody turns up and tells me that Sky Plus is being turned off for a few hours I'm completely livid.

Front of remote – Perfect.)

'WHAT?
SKY'S OFF?
YOU'RE KIDDING?
FOR HOW LONG?
GET THEM ON THE PHONE, NOW!!'

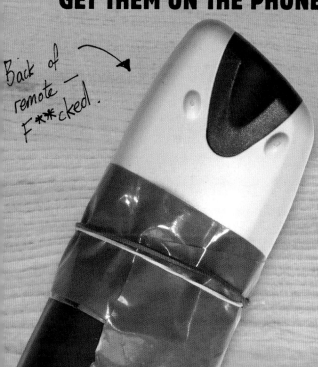

Back of remote – F**cked.

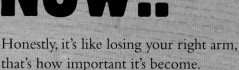

Honestly, it's like losing your right arm, that's how important it's become.

Along with the rest of Britain we had no choice but to 'go digital' with our television signals. This completely messed with my nana's head and no doubt millions of pensioners like her. 'I've just got used to pounds, shillings and pence' was her response to the unavoidable change. In an effort to minimise the frustration and confusion, I decided I'd buy her Sky Plus. Like the adverts say 'Job done, piece of piss.' I thought, she can't go wrong.

I said, 'You'll love this, Nana, it's so easy, you just push that red button there and you can record all your programmes.'

She said, 'Where do I put my tape?'

'Oh no, there's no need for videotapes any more – this has got a hard drive.'

At which she just stared at me blankly. I tried to paint over the cracks by continuing my spiel like a salesman,

'… and it's got live pause, Nana, which means if you want to go to the toilet or have a brew you can just press this button and pause it.'

'But what about everybody else?' she said.

'WHAT? YOU'RE NOT CONTROLLING BRITAIN, THIS IS JUST FOR YOU, HERE. BLOODY HELL YOU'VE NOT GOT THAT KIND OF POWER – WHAT DO YOU EXPECT FOR FORTY POUND A MONTH?'

I had a vision of a couple four hundred miles away in Crawley trying to watch Holby City and the screen pausing. 'I see Mrs Kay's having a slash,' they say, exasperated, and fold their arms in frustration as they wait.

The only thing that bothers me about Sky Plus is the fact that its fast-forward facility has allowed me to be more impatient. My whole life is on x30 speed. I haven't seen an advert for four years now – are DFS still having a sale? Everything is x30, but the only flaw is you can't really control it because it's going so fast, it's all or nothing. So when it finally stops after the adverts the programme is already on. 'Woah! Go back, go back, we're missing it!' my wife shouts with her hands over her eyes. But then you rewind and it shoots back to the beginning of the show. 'Woah! We've seen all this ... go forward, use different speeds, try x6 and then x12.' It would be quicker just to watch the bloody adverts.

You get spoilt with the fast-forward and rewind facility, especially when you are actually watching something that is live – which is a rarity. You find yourself getting frustrated when you try to fast-forward through the adverts and you can't. My children can't comprehend when I tell them, 'No, I can't fast-forward this, it's live.' They just look at me bemused and I can tell they can't quite understand what the concept of 'live' actually means.

Another thing I find to be particularly distressing is when you get a warning sign on screen informing you that you have two programmes recording at once, and because they've clashed you have to choose to delete one before Sky Plus chooses for you. I never know which one to choose. It's like Meryl Streep in

Sophie's Choice: you don't know which one to go for. I mean, it's not so much that I can't decide, it's that it isn't clear which one you are actually choosing. It says select one, but does it mean the one you are selecting is the one you're keeping or the one you're deleting? I'll be hyperventilating on the couch trying to decide. Throwing the remote to my wife I cry, **'QUICK, PICK ONE.'**
She throws it back.
'NO, YOU DO IT, I CAN'T DECIDE.'
And then before you know it Sky Plus has chosen for you and you get 'failed record' on your planner. It causes nothing but panic.

Just like when you find that you've almost used up all of your hard drive memory and you're down to four per cent on your planner.

Now that really tips me over the edge of insanity.

'This is you this,' I say, flicking through page upon page of recordings.

'There's nothing on here that's mine … look, I've got two World's Strongest Man and a Ross Kemp in Bangkok … oh sorry, and a Banged Up Abroad, but then that's your lot,' I say, shaking my head in disgust. 'We've got twenty-seven hours of Twenty-Four here, how the bloody hell has that happened?'

The whole planner is chock-a-block with garbage. 'This is taking all the room up, why have we got Chuggington on series link?' Bloody CBeebies channel; once your children know how to work your Sky Plus you can kiss goodbye to any normal viewing. You can't move on our planner for Fireman 'friggin' Sam and Ben 'bastard' 10.

I try to take a stand. 'I'm deleting some of these … Michael Jackson's funeral? What are you keeping that for?'

'Cause I've not watched that either.'

'The doctor did it★ … delete. Oh yes, that's better, we're back up to forty-eight per cent. I feel cleansed.'

★ Allegedly - for legal reasons

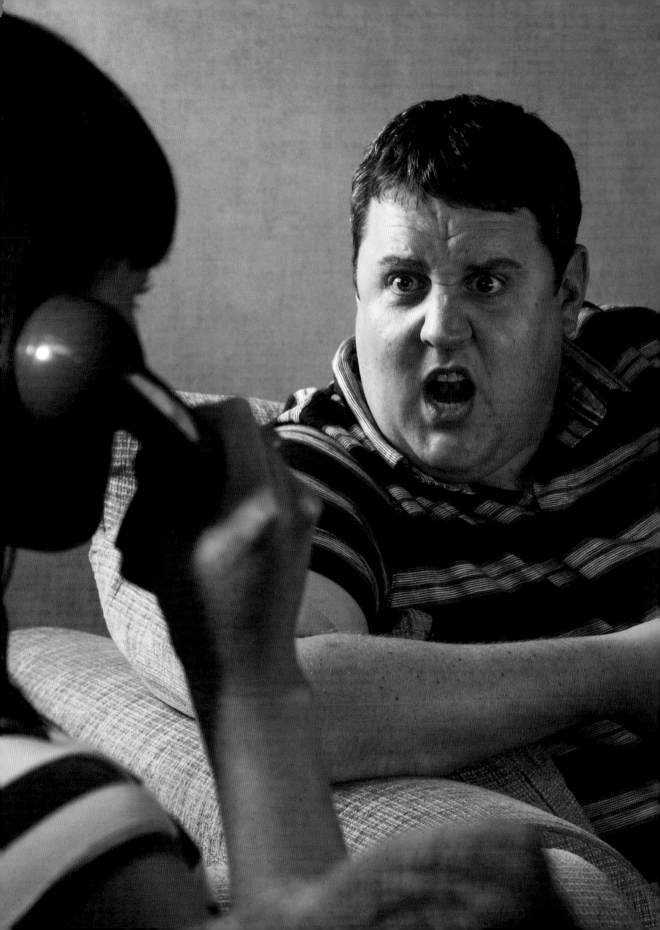

Call it OCD if you like, but you've got to have a tidy planner.

When we do finally sit down to watch something together, my wife's sister rings her up and I've got to stick it on live pause. And sit and wait and wait whilst gesturing, looking at my watch and mouthing the words, 'Come on, tell her you'll call her back', all to no avail. Then at last, after twenty minutes, she says 'bye' and hangs up the phone.

'What did she want?'

'Nothing.'

'NOTHING?!'

I press play and five minutes later the phone rings again. This time it's my mum telling me the ending of the programme we're just about to watch.

'Oh, I didn't expect that twist at the end, I didn't think she'd kill him.'

'MUM!' I shout.

'NO! DON'T SAY ANOTHER WORD AND TELL ME THE END, WE'RE TWENTY MINUTES BEHIND YOU!' The problem with live pause is that everybody is out of sync with everyone else; you don't know who's watching what and when, so you're frightened of ringing and saying anything just in case they're out of sync with you.

I don't know what's live and what's not any more either.

I was watching the ten o'clock news and shouted to my wife, 'Hey, come and look at these miners trapped in Chile.' They'd been out three months; I was watching old news that came on after an episode of Spooks I had on the planner, and I'd forgotten and carried on watching. There I am on the edge of the couch, biting my nails, wondering if they'll ever get out alive, and they're already on the chat-show circuit.

What I find ridiculous is that we've gone from five channels to nine hundred and ninety-nine and yet still I sit there flicking the remote and saying: 'There's nothing on, absolutely sod all on.' Problem is, we've now got more channels than shows to put on them, that's why everything is repeated. I'm watching the same bloody things over and over again.

Take, for example, the other week. I was sat flicking the remote and I happened to land on this American show. There was this bloke in a cowboy hat. He was coming down a staircase in this big mansion, so I sat and watched it. Then an hour later I was flicking again and I landed on this American show,

I saw this bloke in a cowboy hat. He was coming down a staircase in this big mansion, so I sat and watched and thought, 'Hang on, I've just been watching this an hour ago.' Bloody Channel 4+1, ITV1+1 which is technically ITV2 but they've already got an ITV2; in fact they've got a ITV2+1 … where will it end, and why do I need all these choices when all they're showing is the same shit 24/7? The same things come round and round. They've even got a channel called Dave Ja Vu now, Dave Ja Vu: somebody is taking the right royal piss.

I mean, just how many episodes of Scrapheap Challenge can they show in a single day? More4 is the worst one. Every Saturday afternoon without fail you can watch six hours of Grand Designs back to back. SIX HOURS!! And if you miss any you can flick over to More4+1 and catch it again. I mean, I quite like Grand Designs, but six hours? In a row? There's only so many times you can watch two dreamers trying to restore a seventeenth-century castle in the middle of a swamp. Are they stupid? Hello? They've made it out of eco-friendly cardboard they bought on t'internet from Belgium, for God's sake.

GRAND DESIGNS

MORE 4
Everyday - Five times a day

They've gone over budget and Kevin's a right old cow

The presenter, Kevin McCloud, he won't let them get away with anything. He tells it like it is, even when the dreamers are still in earshot. They're stood behind him, full of hope, and he's slagging them off to the camera.

'What are these two playing at? They've spent three years on this money pit, this flat-pack eco-friendly cardboard house, and as you can see the water's still pissing in. They've now gone three hundred and eighty thousand pounds over their original budget and all because SHE wanted to play project manager.'

He's a right old cow. And something else I've noticed is that when Kevin does turn up, three weeks later the wife suddenly discovers she's pregnant again. You watch. Is that a coincidence or what? He's having a pop at her on camera and she's staggering around up the duff in a yellow hard hat, crying.

Supernanny

E4+1 (=E5)
Everyday - Seven times a day

Strawberries and Champagne... but it ain't no picnic for Jo

Supernanny is another show that is repeated continuously. I think she's given herself that title, because I don't know what's so super about stating the obvious. 'Don't give your kids Haribo sweets and have them in bed for Emmerdale.' That's just common sense. But try telling that to a single mum with two hyperactive children screaming the house down.

VOICEOVER: It's three o'clock in the morning and Carol's at her wits' end as her two girls, Strawberry and Champagne, still won't go to sleep.

CAROL: I'm at my wits' end, Supernanny. It's three o'clock in the morning and Strawberry and Champagne still won't go to sleep.

[The sound of girls screaming and laughing comes from the bedroom.]

CAROL: WILL YOU TWO JUST SHUT UP AND GO TO SLEEP!

SUPERNANNY: Don't raise your voice, just talk to them.

VOICEOVER: But then Champagne charges out of the bedroom and decides it's time to play.

CAROL: COME HERE!! I'LL KICK YOUR ARSE.

SUPERNANNY: NO! Just pick her up and put her back to bed. But don't shout and don't give her any eye contact.

VOICEOVER: But just as Carol finally settles Champagne back in bed, Strawberry decides it's now her turn to give her mum the runaround.

CAROL: STRAWBERRY! YOU COME BACK HERE NOW!!

STRAWBERRY: No! Mummy stinks of shit.

[That tips poor Carol straight over the edge. She's knackered chasing Strawberry round the landing while Supernanny stands back watching and shaking her head.]

SUPERNANNY: Don't shout at her, read the rules on the wall. Put her on the naughty step.

CAROL (TO SUPERNANNY): I'LL PUT YOU ON THE NAUGHTY STEP! YOU HAVEN'T EVEN GOT KIDS. YOU WANT TO HELP ME? BABYSIT. I'M GOING TO BED.

The Secret Millionaire

Channel 4
Thursdays (I think)

It's no job too small for multi-millionaire Paul.

The Secret Millionaire, that's another reality show that's on ad infinitum. Mind you, it still makes me cry every week. I only have to see the last five minutes and I'm bawling my eyes out.

VOICEOVER: Paul Davenport runs a multimillion-pound skip-hire business but for the next three weeks he's going to become a secret millionaire.

PAUL DAVENPORT: I've run my own multimillion-pound skip-hire business for thirty years now, man and boy, P.J. Davenport & Son Skip Hire – no job too small, beat any quote or your money back …

VOICEOVER: Paul has to sacrifice his mansion for a shithole bedsit over a halal kebab shop.

PAUL DAVENPORT: Is this it? Is this where I've got to live? Well I'm shocked. I did not expect this at all. I've got to sleep there? [Points to a Z-bed in the corner of the room. Then to some money on a coffee table.] What's this? [Counts it.] Thirty-four pounds fifty. I've got to live off this for a week? I don't know how I'm gonna survive.

End Of Part One.

What did he expect? He's being a secret millionaire; that's the whole point of the programme. It gets worse in Part Two …

VOICEOVER: Paul goes down to a greasy spoon café in an effort to try and find some voluntary work in the local area.

PAUL DAVENPORT: Hello … er … I'm new to the area; it's just me and my camera crew.

I mean, how secret can you be, walking round with two blokes carrying a camera and a six-foot boom mic? Meanwhile Paul's wearing a P.J. Davenport & Son Skip Hire 'No job too small, beat any quote or your money back' T-shirt.

The bloke behind the counter at the greasy spoon tells him there's a church hall up the road that's full of smackheads, so he heads up when he arrives, but – fair play to him – he gets involved. That's usually when he has a bit of a breakdown before the end of Part Three and says something quite powerful to the camera like, 'There but for the grace of God go I', still in his work's T-shirt.

My favourite bit is in Part Four when the millionaire reveals who he really is to the people he's been fooling, I mean helping. He has a shower, a shave and puts on a suit. Next he's knocking on a front door and a startled man answers.

'Paul you're all dressed up, eee ya look smart.'

'I'm here to tell you that I've not been completely honest with you. I'm not who you think I am.'

'You're not from the social, are you?'

'No. I've something to tell you. I'm actually a self-made multi-millionaire, I run a skip-hire business, P.J. Davenport & Son, no job too small, beat any quote or your money back, and I'd like to give you and your disabled wife this cheque for three thousand pounds.'

I'm spitting my tea out at home shouting:

'THREE THOUSAND POUNDS! IS THAT ALL? YOU'VE JUST HAD TWO HUNDRED GRAND'S-WORTH OF FREE ADVERTISING FOR SOD ALL!'

They've opened the floodgates with The Secret Millionaire. Cheeky chancers and smackheads have gotten wise and are shuffling into greasy spoon cafés all over Britain every day with broken camcorders pretending to be 'secret millionaires'.

'Hi, we're new to the area and we're wondering if you could help us out.'

'Oh aye, I've seen this programme [wink, wink to the wife]. We've got a spare room, why don't you come and live with us?'

They spend six months waiting hand and foot on two smackheads. Waiting for the day they'll shower, shave and whip out a chequebook. Poor buggers have got a long wait. The secret millionaires are upstairs, smacked off their tits.

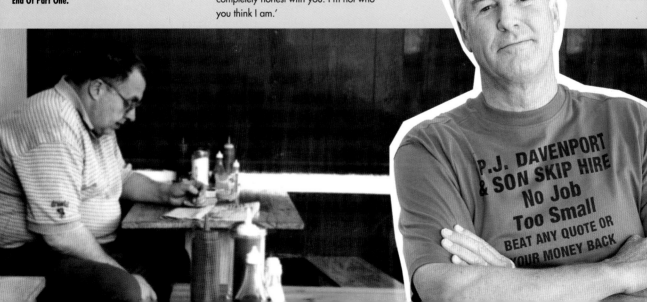

TV's Shite

Embarrassing Bodies

Dr Chris is up to his elbows

Channel 4
Fridays (Before Cheers)

These days it seems as though people will stop at nothing just to get on television. But I think you've got to be completely desperate to go on Embarrassing Bodies. Have you seen that programme? Have those people no shame? The ironic thing is I don't think they're embarrassed about their bodies at all; if they were they wouldn't climb into the back of a lorry in Leeds and drop their drawers on national television.

That's what they do on that show, the programme-makers, they set up these makeshift, walk-in surgeries in the back of trucks and then wait for the dirty, attention-seeking freaks to show up. And trust me, as soon as they see the television cameras they do, in their droves. All sense of pride and dignity lost en route. There was one on the other week, young slip of a girl. 'I've got this condition. I've had it for about six years now and I can't cope any more, it's really embarrassing, people at work are looking at me. I'm mortified 'cause every time I lift my breasts up they fart.'

If you're that embarrassed, why have you just wapped your jugs out in front of a camera crew?

Most of the time the people's problems are just caused by a simple lack of personal hygiene. Give them a bar of soap and they'd run a mile. They don't wash properly, or they've developed a foot fungus because they never change their socks. There was a bloke on it the other week and the diagnosis for his condition was that he'd not been wiping his arse properly. He was fifty. I nearly kicked the television over.

Word of advice, don't watch that show when you're having a take-out. I got a Chinese on the way home and then made the mistake of flicking on Embarrassing Bodies and there was a woman on – her problem? 'My vagina's too big.'

NEW

How To Look Good Naked

"Come on, girls. let's see those tits!"

Channel 4
Tuesday (Same time as Holby)

And if people aren't embarrassed about their bodies, they're trying to figure out How to Look Good Naked. Funny thing is, they never get naked on that programme (I've checked), and all you ever end up seeing is a fifty-odd-year-old dinner lady in a shopping centre with half her arse out while the rest of her is hidden by ostrich feathers.

Gok Wan, what's that fella on? I don't know about you but I'm sure he's gay. Not that I'm bothered. Peter Gay me, some of my best friends and all that. Hey, I'm not homophobic; I'm not scared of my house. I'm only saying that because a straight man wouldn't get away with the stunts Gok pulls – he's obsessed with women's breasts.

'Come on, girls, let's see those tits! Get those tits out for your Auntie Gok! Let's see those melons, busters and bangers.' If I said that to a group of women they'd kick me in the balls and call me a pervert.

Did you see it? It was like a manhole, literally. I was mesmerised and I noticed it was Dr Christian who was straight to the front of queue on that one. He was right up and in there wearing a wet suit and a miner's helmet. It was like a scene from All Creatures Great and Small. My chicken in kung po went straight in the fucking bin.

So this is what we've been reduced to. My theory is that the real reason people go on the show is because they can't get an appointment down at their doctor's because of those bitch receptionists they have answering the phones.

'Hi, I'd like to make an appointment to see the doctor.'

Loud laugh. 'Ha! Doctor? You'll be lucky. Why, what's wrong with you?'

'Well I'd rather tell the doctor.'

'Would you, well you can PISS OFF!'

'Hello, she hung up on me!'

'Hello, is that the doctor's? Can you ask the doctor to come out and see my wife, please, she's very ill.'

'Come out? He can't just come out. You'll have to bring her in.'

'But I can't – she's fitting and foaming at the mouth.'

'Can she come Monday? Oh no, it's a bank holiday, can you bring her in Tuesday?'

'It's all right, I'll drag her down the back of a truck in Leeds.'

CENSORED

COME DINE WITH ME

Channel 4, More 4, E4+1
Too f**king much

Rose has made a cracking Pavlova... To die for.

Come Dine with Me – now I'd sooner stick pins in my eyes than watch that. That's not a cooking show, that's just a set of nosy bastards in your house, looking round your bedrooms while you're downstairs marinating your meat. They asked me to go on Celebrity Come Dine with Me. I said, if you think I'm having Brian Blessed and 'H' from Steps rooting through my cupboards, you've got another think coming. That's how they caught

Fred and Rose West, on Come Dine with Me. It was the pilot episode; they've never shown it. Which is a shame because Rose made a cracking pavlova – to die for, apparently.

Along with the weekly Grand Designs-athon on More4, if you happen to miss Come Dine with Me you can catch it again every Saturday afternoon on Channel 4, when they show five episodes in a row or, failing that, again on Channel 4+1. Basically what I'm

saying is, you can run but you can't hide.

And if you miss them on TV, you can now catch your favourite show on t'internet, thanks to 4OD, ITV Player and BBC iPlayer. We've got nothing but choices. You can even download them to your th'iPhone and watch them on your way to work. Your battery only lasts nine minutes, but you can watch them nonetheless and leave your phone on charge for the rest of the day.

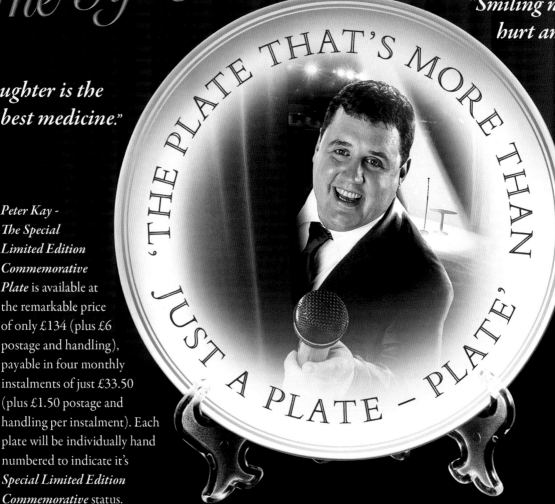

I don't know about you but my whole life is on charge. I can't sleep at night for green flashing lights. The bedroom looks like a spaceship.

Everybody's banging on about not wasting electricity and taking care of the environment, and yet they're still bringing out more gadgets that you have to plug in and charge up every day of the week.

I'm a bugger for charging my phones. I turn up at friends' houses.

'Hi, it's great to see you, thanks for having us round … by the way, have you got a charger for a Nokia? I'm flashing low battery. It's the one with the small hole. I need some juice.' Talk about pig ignorant. But your phone is your life. If you leave it at home by accident you feel like you've lost your left arm or that you're missing out on something important. Everybody needs to be contactable 24/7 and yet nobody's really got anything to say.

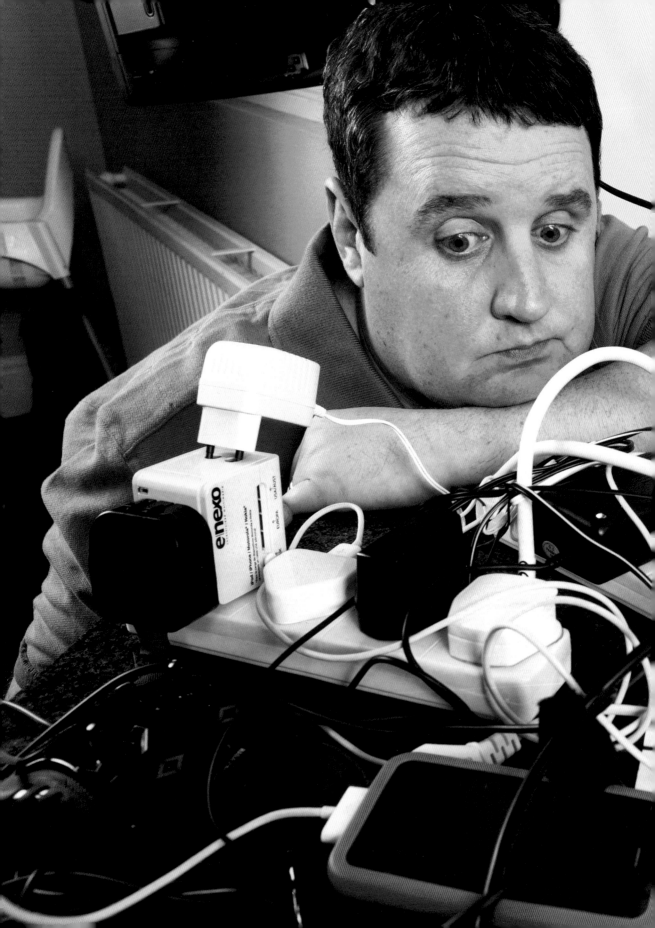

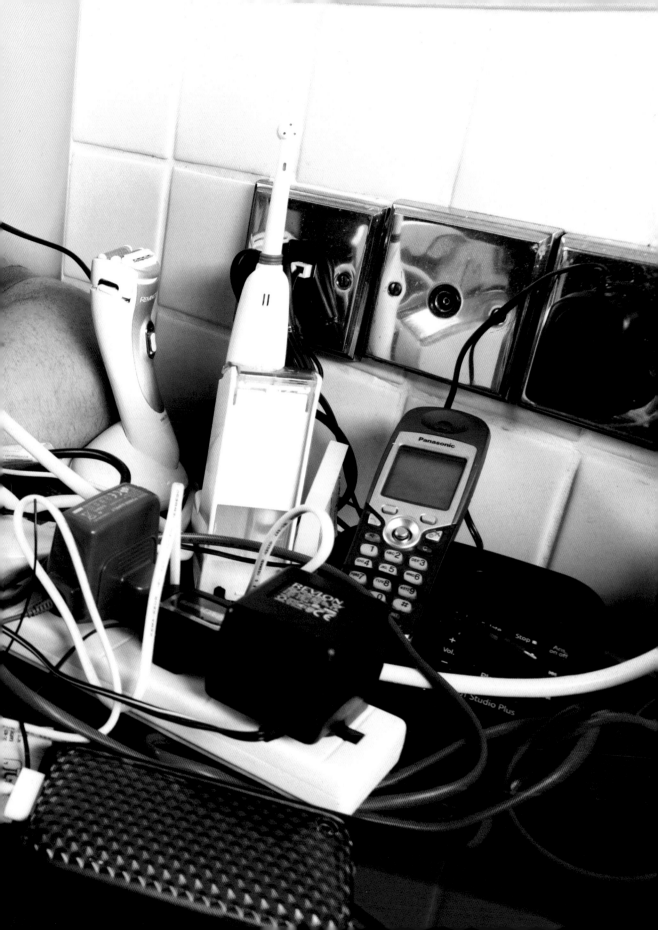

Before we all had mobiles, when you arranged to meet a friend you did it in advance and that was that. There was none of this texting, 'I'm running L8' or 'Be there in 2 minutes' horseshit. They just had to wait and if you didn't turn up they'd have to go to a payphone and ring you to see where you were and by the time they got back you'd been and gone.

I've got that bad with texting now I don't even give my mum three rings any more. When I get home safe, I just text her the words: '3 rings'. That's how lazy I've become.

I got one of those silent calls the other week. You know the ones that freak you out where they don't speak. Only difference was I could hear somebody breathing on the other end of the phone.

'Hello? Hello?'

Nothing, just the sound of some psycho breathing.

'Hello, I know there's somebody there, I can hear you breathing … It's okay – two can play at this game, dickhead.'

I thought if they want a war, they've got a war. So I sat on the stairs and waited and waited and still they said nothing, just that breathing.

After about forty-five minutes it had really started to freak me out, so I surrendered and hung up. I put the phone back in its holster in the kitchen and decided to do some bits. You know, empty the dishwasher, bleach my cloths, that type of thing. But I was still curious so I went over to the phone and lo and behold there was now a dialling tone, the other person had finally hung up. Quickly I dialled 1471 to identify the caller's number and a mobile number came up, so I pressed 3 to be connected and after a few seconds my mobile phone began to ring in my trouser pocket. What an arsehole.

I realised that when I'd bent down to put my slippers on in the bedroom I must have accidentally dialled my home number from my mobile. So there I was, sat on the stairs for forty-five minutes listening to myself breathing, via satellite. That call ended up costing me thirty-eight quid.

KEEPING A NATION HEALTHY since 1922

KAY EFF SEE

KAY EFF SEE

KAY EFF SEE

Not only are we spoilt for choice when it comes to TV channels, but we're spoilt when it comes to choices of food these days too. I think we only ever went out for a meal twice when I was growing up. Once for my holy communion and then again when my dad got his compensation money through. Both times it was to the same carvery up the road.

Now families eat out all the time, and I'm not just talking about the McDonald's drive-thru. Children have got much more cultured palates now, with many more choices including Italian, Chinese, Indian, Spanish, Mexican. I'd never tasted chicken in black bean sauce until I was in my early thirties and the first time I had a peshwari naan was just three weeks ago. It was completely overwhelming.

With all these choices, it's no wonder we've all put on a bit of weight in the last ten years or so – even I've developed a bit of a veranda over the toyshop. I have to be honest, I've always struggled with food, mainly in keeping it out of my mouth. And at the end of the day **YOU ARE WHAT YOU EAT. I'M A WALNUT WHIP.**

I do try to look after myself. I joined a gym, but even that tipped me over the edge. All those people driving around trying to find a parking space near the front door. Why they don't just park down the road and walk up is beyond me. But no, they always have to get a space right up close to the building before they then spend the next hour and a half walking on a bloody treadmill.

I felt intimidated in the gym environment. It wasn't the exercising in Lycra or the blokes lifting weights to 'Eye of the Tiger', it was the metrosexuals coming up to me in the changing rooms later, stark bollock naked, wanting to chat. I didn't know where to put my eyes. I mean, would you ever?

'SO, PETE, YOU BUSY? WHAT ARE YOU UP TO?'

'WELL, RIGHT NOW I'M DRYING MY BALLS IF YOU DON'T MIND.'

That put me off going and I was doing okay as well. I used to go three times a week and I felt exhilarated after an hour's workout; then I'd fall on my sword and call into the cafe on the way out for a tuna baguette with chips – well, I had worked up quite an appetite after all.

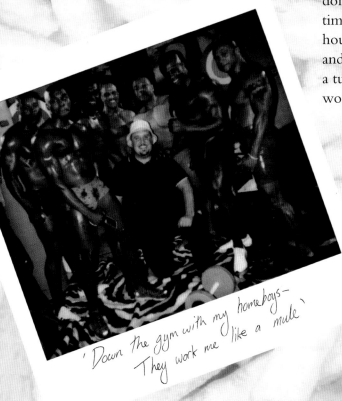

'Down the gym with my homeboys – They work me like a mule'

I've tried those workout DVDs too, and spent many hours rolling around on the front-room floor clutching two tins of beans for weights. I borrowed a Rosemary Conley video once from my Auntie Pat – she wasn't my real auntie, of course. She was just somebody my mum did water aerobics with every other Thursday. Anyway, I put the video on and was getting into it. I was following Lynne. She was the woman in the corner of the screen who'd just had a 'major' operation and was taking it easy. If you fancied a gentler workout you could mirror her exercises. I was still sweating buckets and was just getting my breath back when Rosemary casually said, 'Right, now we've warmed up, let's start our workout.' Eject!! I was absolutely knackered.

A few weeks ago I got desperate and had a look in the paper. I found a local aerobics class and decided to go along.

I mustn't have read the advert right because I was the youngest one there and the only bloke. I tried to keep my head down at the back, hiding behind a woman who was clearly in her seventies. Cath was leading the class at the front. I mean it was hardly 'high energy' – all we were doing was walking forwards and backwards to Betty Boo – 'Doin' the Do'. Then Cath cranked it up a gear with a few low squats and Dizzee Rascal's 'Bonkers', which came completely out of left field.

'COME ON EVERYBODY, LET'S GO BONKERS!'

she shouted from the front over her squat thrusts. You know, even though I was mortified at first, I slowly started to relax and get into it. I certainly got my £3.20's-worth, and by the end of the class I was shattered. I'm going again next week if you want to come.

Jamie

Gordon

Kojak

I blame the influx of all these cooking shows on TV for the weight gain. They just make you want to eat. We've got Jamie's 30-Minute Meals (which actually take just over an hour, and that's with a Kenwood Chef and a wet tea towel under my chopping board). We've got Gordon Ramsay effing and blinding and jeffing at the staff at a Harvester. And now the king of all cooking shows has made a triumphant return to our screens, MasterChef. People can't get enough of it. Who'd have thought it would become such a success after all those years ago with Lloyd Grossman, wedged in between The Clothes Show and Songs of Praise on a Sunday afternoon?

Now they've given it a makeover with fast editing and dramatic music. You'd think you were watching CSI MasterChef the way they put it across. Psychologically, I'm on the edge of my seat, and all they're doing is boiling some broccoli stems. And as for the rubbish they talk – well, they've taken it to a completely new level.

'Hmmmm, oh yeah, now that dessert is a piece of heaven! I'm not tasting it, this dessert is tasting me. It's earthy, it's strong, it's refreshing, but above all it's one of the finest mint Viennettas I've ever had. You've defrosted this with true perfection and I'd like to kiss your mother and father for giving birth to you.'

I've always wanted to go on there and cook something. 'Today, Greg, I'm going to be making potato and leek Cup a Soup with croutons. For mains we'll be having instant mash made with boiled water, accompanied by Shopping giant beans and mini-meatballs, and for dessert I'll be preparing Elmlea rice pudding with a blob of red jam, stir it up and make it pink.' I'd clean up and win it hands down.

But I have to admit these cooking shows have opened my eyes to a whole new culinary world I didn't know existed. I'd never even heard of oregano, now I've got two jars of it in my cupboard, and don't get me started on fennel seeds.

You can't move in my fridge for chorizo sausage and Parma ham. We've suddenly found ourselves in this Come Dine with Me culture. Gone are the days of going down to the local pub for a few jars. Now people have dinner parties to organise and competitions to cook for each other. Which I'm all in favour of – the problem is that we haven't got a dining-room table. We only used it on public holidays and for the occasional séance, so we eventually sacrificed it for the extra space. And you can't really have a dinner party round a wallpaper table, so that leaves us with the breakfast bar as the only option. It can take five at a push, which is not exactly Dallas with everyone's knees banging together.

Watching what food you eat can be difficult, so I decided to try doing my shopping online so I could monitor just what I was buying and make sure it wasn't any unhealthy rubbish. So you go on t'internet and you book your slot. Then you start your shop, which takes ages because you've got to troll through pages and pages of stuff, and then after three hours you finally place your order. The problem is when they do eventually come to deliver your shopping they sometimes bring you swaps. Like the time I ordered Angel Delight and he brought me Cillit Bang. I thought, How do they go together? Is there something I was missing? And all my fruit and veg was rotten. It was literally dripping out of the bottom of the carrier bag, dissolving. I thought 'What am I going to do with this? I'm not making Hooch.' I tried t'internet shopping once and then I was straight back to the big shop. Every Friday we go, my mum and me. We park in the parent and child spot. And why not? I'm with my mum – they don't have an age limit on it.

Friday is a really bad day to do a big shop, not only because the supermarket is usually packed, but also because Friday is officially the start of the weekend, so any willpower is lost in the heady anticipation of the days ahead.

I'm useless and always come home with bags full of complete crap that's neither requested nor required. Like the other Friday when I got excited and came home with a six-pack of Bird's Super Mousse, a giant tub of hot chocolate and a rack for the bath. I only went in for a toastie loaf.

Shop when you're hungry, that's my advice – the amount of shit you buy when you're starving is incredible. I've always been a sucker for the chocolate aisle. I find it hard to pass it by. I genuinely try, but whatever trolley I get, it always seems to have a will of its own and pulls me there. I'll chuck just about everything in: triple chocolate cookies, mint Viscounts, packets of Penguins, KP Choc Dips, Blue Ribands, limited edition KitKats. Now I find it impossible to turn down any limited edition chocolate.

'Hey, they're limited edition, we've got to get them, quick! You don't know how long they're going to be around.' Well, that's my excuse anyway.

The only thing that gets me down about doing a big shop on a Friday is that the checkouts are always so busy. You try and assess which queue looks the shortest. Scanning up and down the line of tills, seeing which numbers are lit up. When I spy one I push my way over, only to inevitably hear those infuriating words: 'Sorry, I'm closing now.' To which I want to scream, **'WELL TURN YOUR SODDING TILL LIGHT OFF THEN,'** but instead of course I just say, 'Oh, don't worry' and walk on. 'Happy to help', my arse.

I'm ashamed to admit I sometimes resort to underhand tactics. Like shuffling up to somebody who's already in a queue, then deliberately standing behind them holding half a pint of semi-skimmed milk and giving them my pathetic eyes, like the cat from Shrek 2. More often than not they will eventually take pity on me.

'IS THAT ALL YOU'VE GOT?'

I give them a sad nod.

'OK. YOU CAN GO IN FRONT.'

'THANKS, MUUUUUUM!!'

And then my mum will come hurtling around the corner, pulling and pushing two trolleys piled high with the big shop.

Now they've got those self-service checkouts where you can scan an item yourself. The only flaw with this method, I find, is trust. Who's watching? You can rob them blind if you fancy; you can even make the beeping sound yourself and stuff the shopping down your trousers. But it always ends up taking just as long as queuing up because I can never figure out how to work them or find the bar code for scanning.

When I do the big shop I always forget to bring my bag for life so I have to buy another one. I've got thirteen bags for life now – how long am I going to live? I've no choice but to get one, though, because I've gone and left the other twelve outside in the boot of the car in that fine rain that soaks you through and I can't be

arsed going to get them. That's the way society has got me now. I've been brainwashed into being environmentally friendly. I'm continually racked with guilt and I seem to spend most of my time these days walking to and from our recycling bins with an armful of plastic bottles, milk cartons and cans.

PEA JUICE is running down my arm while the lid from a tin of baked beans slices my hand open. I look like a prisoner of war in a T-shirt and jogging bottoms. In an effort to clear my conscience, I tip the lot in, only to return to the kitchen and find even more on the side. 'Christ, I've just taken a load out.' So back I go again. It's never-ending, this recycling.

We've got so many different coloured wheelie bins now that I lose track of what's supposed to go where. 'Is blue for plastic or paper? Brown's garden waste? Is green not garden waste? Well what the hell is purple for?' Honestly, I can't keep up, and I can never remember what bin we're supposed to put out on a weekly basis. I usually just copy the old couple up the road because basically they live for putting their bins out. It's the main focus of their entire week. The problem is they're either demented or colour-blind, because our purple bin hasn't been emptied for the past four weeks. It's started to stink. I'm going to have to fly-tip it if the council don't empty it soon.

'OLD PEOPLE LIVE FOR PUTTING THEIR BINS OUT'

So I get home from the supermarket and begin the rigmarole of putting the groceries away. Fifteen minutes later and I can't shut the cupboard door for jam Wagon Wheels. It literally is choco-block (see what I did there?).

'I'll start Monday,' I say. That's my weekend mantra. 'I'll get the next three days out of the way and then I'll start Monday.'

The only problem with that is that there's fifty-two Mondays in a year.

I play out entire conversations in my mind. I get into bitter arguments with myself. They'll start with something like: 'It's come to something when I can't have a bit of chocolate at the weekend and treat myself.' Then it slowly escalates to, 'It's come to something when I can't have a Chinese takeaway on a Saturday night.' Next thing you know I'm trying to compromise by having a full English for breakfast with a Slim•Fast shake.

'I'LL START MONDAY.'

Monday comes and I start with the obligatory detox: a glass of boiled water with a squirt of Jif lemon. Followed by a bowl of Special K.

Then I have a migraine and a whinge to whoever will listen about, 'I can't go on like this any longer', and I've only been on the detox since Jeremy Kyle. It's not even Monday lunchtime. I have my second bowl of Special K to try and drop a jean size. By the end of This Morning I'm stood in front of the bedroom mirror, side on, checking to see if I've lost any weight.

It actually sounds pretty pathetic when I write it down like this, but round and round I go, week in week out. Start a diet Monday and by Wednesday I'm like a junkie, hunting around for anything that even resembles a treat. I'm not so cocky about my cupboard full of chocolate treats then. By this time I'm desperate and stood on a chair in the kitchen checking to see if any chocolate has worked its way to the back of the cupboard. 'There must be something in here … Rich Tea Fingers, crap', and then I stretch into the dark, hidden recesses of the back of the now nearly bare cupboard. Just a stray Mini Egg will do, anything. And there it is, nestled between a packet of Snack a Jacks and an out-of-date jar of Reggae Reggae sauce, a jam Mini Roll, slightly squashed, I see, but who cares. A jam Mini Roll is like a banquet on a Wednesday in our house.

'COME QUICK!
I'VE FOUND A JAM MINI ROLL.'

Manna from heaven. It doesn't even touch the sides when it reaches my mouth.

You know what I also hate? And yes, it's right up there with wire coat hangers and the Go Compare man. It's when you see a tin of Celebrations on the side and you go over to open it only to discover it's a sewing kit! I really hate that. Talk about an anti-climax. I rip off the lid for a sly tiny Mars and find thread, buttons and Velcro. It messes with your mind. My mum has had the same tin of Roses for over twenty-six years and I fall for it every time. I check the coast is clear, quietly prise off the lid and find plasters, Paracetamols and bandages. What's sad is that I still always have a shufty just in case there's a Caramel Barrel lurking under the antihistamines.

I do love going to my mum's, though. She always takes pity on me. She did it today. She told me I needed to lose some weight and then in the next breath asked me if I wanted a bacon and sausage butty. She's dynamite. We go up every week for Sunday dinner because you really can't beat your own mum's cooking, especially when it's a roast dinner. I think it's nothing short of magic what she can produce in her kitchen. And the taste – well, she'd win every series of MasterChef hands down with her cooking.

I'd tip my hat to her, if I wore one. Because making a Sunday dinner takes real skill – trust me, I've tried. I'd have been lost in the kitchen if it hadn't been for Aunt Bessie. That lady really is the saviour of the Sunday roast. If you've not seen the Aunt Bessie range down the supermarket then you're missing a treat. And she does the lot now: Yorkshire puddings, roast potatoes, honey-glazed parsnips, cauliflower cheese. She's even tried her hand at sticky toffee pudding. I honestly don't know how she finds the time.

SHE MUST BE RUSHED OFF HER FEET, THE POOR COW

– it's no wonder she's got red cheeks on the front of that bag. I think Aunt Bessie should be recognised in the New Year's Honours list, because for me she's done more for Sunday dinners than any of these so-called TV chefs.

I appreciate that organising and preparing a Sunday roast can be tough, I just wish my mum didn't get so stressed while she's doing it. I try to help her by laying the table and pouring the drinks. Occasionally I even try to help her dish the food out, but I struggle, as, quite simply, I've not got asbestos hands. Have you noticed that all mums have got asbestos hands? My mum can juggle fire without the sticks. Some plates can be above eighty degrees in the oven, but she'll pick them up like they're made of paper. She'd put Red Adair to shame.

Usually any efforts I make to help her are thwarted and she bellows,

Sunday PM

'GET OUT!
I DON'T NEED ANYBODY'S HELP, JUST LEAVE ME ALONE'

in a northern Irish accent sounding not dissimilar, at that point, to the Right Hon. Rev.

Tuesday AM

Ian Paisley. So over the years I've slowly come to terms with the fact that my mum prefers to be left alone when she's dishing out her Sunday dinner. I'll gently retreat to the front room where the rest of the family chuckle to themselves as we listen to her perform her gastronomic stock-take.

'Right I've got my meat, my roast potatoes, my boiled potatoes, my cauliflower cheese, my carrots, my broccoli, my Yorkshire puddings, my peas … PEAS? Oh no, where are the peas? I've lost the peas,' she panics – they're nowhere to be seen. Until two days later when she finds them in the microwave lounging in a small plastic bowl. Panic over.

One of the rituals I love most at my mum's on a Sunday is when we have the occasional birthday tea. It doesn't even matter if your birthday falls midweek, the festivities are scooped up to the nearest Sunday and suddenly you find you're in for a big surprise – or not as the case may be. It was my nephew's birthday recently. He was fifteen. I couldn't believe it. It doesn't seem two minutes since I was stood with him in my fleece queuing up to watch Flubber. Now he's fifteen I can no longer get away with Sellotaping pound coins into his birthday card. He now has a bigger and better birthday list, with things like games for his Xbox and his Wii.

Wiis are amazing; I never thought I'd see my nana waterskiing at eighty-nine. She's phenomenal, kayaking around the front room with her remote as a paddle. We've certainly come a long way since Frogger. One of my favourites is Guitar Hero. Have you been on that? Not that you can answer. It's an incredible invention, which I would have loved growing up. Then I used to put on my dad's LPs and play rock star in my bedroom. I'd put on my dad's sunglasses, my mum's block heels and make-up and sing into the back of the Hoover, pretending it was a microphone. Now come on, everybody used to do that. Didn't they?

I used to use my dad's shovel as a guitar because I thought it looked and felt better than a tennis racket. Not that I was allowed to use a tennis racket after I set fire to R Julie's in the back yard imitating Jimi Hendrix during Wimbledon fortnight. My dad would go searching for his shovel while I was upstairs jumping off my bedding box like Pete Townshend. BANG!! I'd hit my bedroom floor with a thud, causing the whole house to shake and my dad to wail up through the ceiling,

'CHRIST ALMIGHTY BOY! ARE YOU COMING THROUGH THAT CEILING OR WHAT? WE'RE TRYING TO WATCH TENKO DOWN HERE. THEY ESCAPE TONIGHT. IF I COULD BLOODY HEAR IT.'

But I'd rock on regardless, giving it my all. Throwing the records on to my midi hi-fi turntable with twin cassette decks and a powerful hi-speed dubbing facility. Two of my favourites were Status Quo 12 Gold Bars and Queen's Greatest Hits. I loved Queen and used to parade around my bedroom swapping between Brian May and Freddie Mercury. I remember borrowing my mum's leotard once. A bright white one that she used to wear for aerobics. I chose it because it was slightly similar to the one Freddie wore in the video to 'Flash'. I even drew a big red flash down it in red felt tip. Then my mum went mad when I stuck it in the washing basket and it turned my school shirts pink.

'Look at my good leotard, you destroyed it. Bloody big red flash down the front – how am I supposed to wear that for Jazzercise now? You've misshaped it, it's ruined.'

'Don't stop me now, I'm having such a good time, I'm having a ball. Oh you're such a killer queen, Mum … ' I mumbled as I legged it up the stairs to my room before I got a clip round the ear. Happy days.

Anyway where was I? Oh yes, my nephew's birthday tea. So the ritual is basically always the same. Just as we've finished our Sunday dinner, my mum starts to clear the plates whilst discreetly nodding and winking at R Julie to come and help her. Then they both slope off into the kitchen, leaving us all to listen to their antics as they loudly whisper to each other.

'Where are the matches?' and, 'Have you got the candles?'

'They're in the card drawer.'

My mum has a card drawer. She's got everything in there. You name the card and she's got it, Happy Thirtieth, Happy Hanukkah, Just Passed Your Driving Test – she'd give Clinton's a run for their money with the stuff she's got in that drawer. Bottle bags, wrapping paper; she's even got the present tags to put on them, too. She makes her own, she's craft mad. Cutting up her old cards with her corrugated scissors. I give her a Christmas card and she'll say, 'Thank you. Oh, that'll make a nice tag for next year.' She can't wait to cut it up.

'Bloody hell, Mum! You've not even put it on the mantelpiece yet.' Being her son, my cards automatically get pride of place on the mantelpiece over the fireplace. My mum has a tiering system for cards. Main family goes on the fireplace next to the clock. That's why I'm not keen on these new flatscreen tellys – they're too thin and you can't sit your cards on top.

Other family, like cousins and friends, they get relegated to the bottom of the fireplace near the grate. You know you're not so popular when you discover you're next to a lamp on a side table behind the mansize tissue box. Mind you, it could be worse, my uncle Nobhead has been behind the spider plant on the windowsill for years.

Meanwhile, back at the birthday tea, after what seems like an eternity of painful silence, my mum's hand eventually appears around the side of the door and we all watch as she gropes down the wall for the light switch. Click, and we're plunged into darkness, apart from the distant glow of candles reflecting off the cupboards in the kitchen. Then my mum and R Julie both emerge from the darkness singing 'Happy Birthday' and carrying a chocolate caterpillar cake from Asda with Smarties for eyes. And then we've all got to react enthusiastically and surprised like it's never ever happened before.

Then the birthday girl or boy is told to close their eyes, make a wish and blow out the candles. If you've got small children they always have to blow out the candles too. 'I want a go, I want a go.' So you've got to relight them several times just to keep the peace as they each take a turn in blowing out the candles. Unless you get those relightable candles; my mum got some by mistake and the children slowly keeled over one by one. We were chatting and never realised, till they were all in a heap on the floor.

'Would you like a slice of cake?'

'ER . . . I'LL HAVE SOME WHEN YOU'VE WIPED THAT TOP LAYER OF SPIT OFF IT, PLEASE. I DON'T WANT TO GET HEPATITIS B.'

Occasionally we go out for birthday tea, which I'm not really keen on as usually it means we've got to invite other members of the family, mainly me uncle Nobhead and his wife and I don't mean my auntie Sandra, oh no. They've split up, it's all kicked off. I'm talking about his new bride, Nu Fang Dow, from Thailand. He got her off eBay (I told you you could get anything). DHL had her for four weeks because he lost his card. They had to get a neighbour to sign for her in the end. Then my uncle Nobhead came home from the airport and found her sat behind the wheelie bin reading the new Next catalogue. He was so over the moon with her that he even hired a billboard on the main high street showing off their wedding photo. My auntie Sandra was mortified when she saw it driving to Zumba, and skidded her Clio off the road and straight through the window of You Can Call Me Halal.

So there's always an atmosphere when they come now. Plus he drinks too much and gets too loud. Like the time it was his birthday tea and he insisted on going to Frankie & Benny's because they were doing a two-for-one with free balloons and if you tell the assistant manager it's your birthday they dim the lights during dessert and all the waiters come out singing 'Happy Birthday' to a CD. The one where they substitute the person's name for an extra 'happy birthday'. It's excruciating because everybody is encouraged to join in, and when it's packed they're doing it every four minutes. Anyway, Uncle Nobhead pounced on this young waitress for a birthday kiss and was escorted off the premises shouting **'GET THAT FRANKIE AND BENNY OUT HERE NOW, I'LL KICK THEIR HEADS IN.'**

We've never been back.

If we do have to go out for birthday tea, I prefer it if we go Italian because I get free garlic bread – that's one of my job's perks. It usually takes about ten minutes before a waiter will come over with some garlic bread and stand, and chuckle, and wait, and chuckle, until finally I'll acknowledge what he's just done and say,

'WHAT'S THIS? GARLIC? BREAD? GARLIC? AND BREAD? TOGETHER? IT'S THE FUTURE?'

He finds this hysterical. 'That's right, the chef he seen your DVD and he told me to give you this – free garlic? bread? It's sa da future, no? Ha, ha.'

At least we all get free garlic? bread? That's why my new catchphrase is 'Plas? Ma? Seventy-inch? Plas? Ma? On my wall for free?' Well you never know, do you?

One thing that I've noticed about eating out as a family is that nobody ever complains. Well, they complain to each other, but God forbid they'd ever complain to a member of staff.

'That couple are on their main meal and they came in after us; we've only just got our starters and look they're on their bloody main meal, it's a disgrace.'

Then a waiter comes over. 'Is everything all right, madam?'

'Oh yes, lovely thanks, special,' and then as soon as they're out of earshot. 'Shithole. I'm not coming here again.'

'Apparently it's changed hands.'

I've always loved that expression. 'It's changed hands.'

Then when they do bring the food, why are the plates always so hot? And they actually apologise for it when they put them down, holding them with a napkin.

'There you go and please watch the plates, they're very hot. They might burn you.'

I want to say, 'Well take them back. Jesus Christ, I've got children here! Is it absolutely necessary for the plates to be scalding? Surely we won't die of malnutrition if you just wait a few minutes and let them cool down a bit? I'd rather have lukewarm food than third-degree burns.' But of course I never do. I just smile like everybody else and say, 'Lovely thanks,' because nobody ever complains.

We always swap with each other's food. 'Oh, yours looks nice.'

'Here, have a taste,' and then food will be passed over the table from one plate to another.

'Oh yes, it is nice that, I wish I'd have got that. Here, try some of mine,' and then even more food is passed across the table. Before you know it there's gravy dripped everywhere. 'Here, have some chips, they've given me too many chips,' and then fistfuls of chips will come over the table and on to your plate. They're like pigs at trough, bits of food everywhere.

The thing that surprises me, after all that, is how fussy people are when it comes to sharing each other's cutlery. That's just crossing the line for some reason. 'Here, take your fork back. I don't want your fork.' People are also very

finicky about sharing bottles. Sometimes wiping the top clean with their hands suspiciously before taking a drink, if at all.

I had a dodgy experience with that a few years ago in Gran Canaria. I was out on the street one night with a few friends and I found myself to be incredibly thirsty. Perhaps it was the dry heat or the fact that I'd had gammon for tea, who knows, but either way I was spitting feathers and needed to quench my thirst quickly. When my 'friend' Paul handed me a big bottle of Pepsi, I gratefully snatched it out of his hand and swigged it back.

'It's warm that,' I said, slightly perturbed.

To which he replied, 'I know,' laughing, 'I just got it out of that bin over there,' and pointed to a litter bin swarming with flies. I just spewed up there and then, which only seemed to add to his merriment. In fact I was still spitting into the toilet back at the hotel at three o'clock in the morning.

So you've had your birthday meal and you reach that point where you have to make the decision whether to 'join the pudding club' or not and have a dessert. As you scan round the table for an accomplice, bizarrely nobody can seem to make eye contact with you. It's as if the thought of dessert has become a sign of great weakness in modern society. I usually take the plunge, justifying it by saying, 'Well, it's come to something when you can't celebrate someone else's birthday without having a dessert. I'll start Monday,' and sure enough everybody else falls into line, except for one awkward arse who orders a cheeseboard instead – that's usually my uncle Nobhead and yet he still always manages to nick a spoon so he can steal a bit of everybody's dessert. Now that drives me crazy; in fact I once stabbed the back of his hand with my fork in a Berni Inn for doing that. I was eight years old but he's still never forgiven me.

Sure enough, the waiter will bring me a complimentary slice of cheesecake.

'HEY, CHEESE? CAKE?
A CAKE OF CHEESE?'

'Plas? Ma?'

But it's lost on him as it's not in the context of this book you're reading and hasn't yet been established as a catchphrase.

After the dessert and coffee with mints we're all usually stuffed and delight in describing to each other triumphantly how we are.

'Lordy, I'm as full as a tick.'
'I'm as full as a bull's bum.'

It's the complete opposite to the start of the meal when all we could do was tell each other how hungry we were.

'I could eat a horse.'
'I could eat a scabby pig.'

Full, and with the flutterings of an indigestion that will no doubt find me sat on the edge of my bed at four in the morning, sobbing to myself and mumbling those all too familiar words 'never again', I eventually manage to catch the waiter's eye and ask for the bill in the only way I know how, by using the international gesture of the bill. As you'll know, this involves miming writing a signature in mid-air with an invisible pen. It works anywhere in the world and never lets you down. The other option is the little pad, where you pretend to fold open a writing pad and write on that, but it isn't half as much fun or usually as effective. Either way, the waiter eventually comes over with the machine for your secret PIN number and then turns away.

Pizza the Action
Stitch-Mi-Lane, Bolton BL3 YHG
01204 6132546
www.pizzatheaction.com

Table No 7	People 12	Date 11/6
Your Order		**Price**
Doughballs x 7	Peroni	
Spare Ribs x 2	Pimms	
Penne Panna	White wine	
Spag Bol	Britvic 55	
Bruschetta	Half Becks	
Fill Steak	J20 Oran/Passion	
Carbornara	Lrg Still Water	£338.76
Lasagne	Bud	
Salad	Speckled Hen	
Garlic? Bread? x 11	Coke	

VAT NO. 878767

A word of advice: if you're asking for the bill, then basically you're the one taking the responsibility for paying for it. Be careful, I've had some lovely meals that have gone tits-up as soon as the bill has arrived. The mood just seems to change, with everybody becoming awkward and embarrassed about money. But what are you to do?

You can split it straight down the middle. This isn't a bad option, but somebody always gets the hump because they didn't have wine.

You can painfully try and account for each individual food order. But this can take hours and I've experienced first hand the stubborn rage of two people, nose to nose, arguing over the cost of a dough ball (I know because, shamefully, I was one of the two).

Or, and this is undoubtedly the best option, somebody can simply pick up the bill on everybody's behalf. Unfortunately this only usually occurs when you see a flying pig against a blue moon.

As soon as you start to work out the bill, that's when the fun starts, or rather stops. It can easily deteriorate into a Maths lesson unless one of the guests has a calculator on their th'iPhone. I always find there's at least one gobby girl with control issues who likes grabbing the bull by the horns.

'Right, so splitting it twelve ways makes twenty-eight pounds and twenty-three pence EACH!!'

'Here, there's sixty pounds from us.' A couple hand their money over.

'Sixty pound going in!! … WAIT, I owe you three fifty-four change.'

'No you're all right, take it as a tip.'

'I've included the tip already. Can you wait? I've no change yet … Has anybody got any shrapnel?' she shouts down the table.

'Can we pay part-card part-cash?'

There's always someone who wants to do that. She glares at them.

'You can if you want to ruin my system. Dickhead.'

And there's always a really nice girl who's hardly had anything to eat but still wants to pay the same as everybody else.

'Hey, what are you doing? Take that back, you didn't have any wine, or a starter, or a even a main meal. You only had a breadstick and then you were in the toilets for an hour. And it's your birthday so take that back,' Gobby cow says, passing her money back to her.

'OK, so that's seventy-two, seventy-three … wait, I'm still short. Someone's not paid. Who's not paid yet? … They've what? They've gone?'

That always happens. There's always a tight-arse couple who say they have to get back for babysitter and slope off early without paying. You've gotta watch that. She won't let that go. That'll be the talk of the works canteen on Monday and it'll fester for a full twelve months until they're all out again. Gobby cow has a few too many wines and, 'So, are you going to pay this year or are you going to sneak off early like you did last time?' And that's it

– next thing you know the table's gone over and the police are on their way. I've never been on a works do yet where there's not been a fight. That includes my own works dos and I'm self-employed.

It's the same every Christmas, just me on a sixty-seat coach fighting with the driver, and I still have to send the hat round for him. I had a right character for a driver last year, Terry from Liverpool. Mixed-race bloke with a thick Scouse accent and a handlebar moustache. He was like a cross between Craig Charles and Lemmy (if you can imagine such a thing). I'd just had a night out on my own for the festive season, casino, strip club, usual and even though I was the only passenger on board he still insisted on regaling me with all of his coach rules. They're a bugger for the rulebook, coach drivers.

'WE'VE GOT A CHEMICAL TOILET ON BOARD BUT IF YOU'RE GOING TO USE IT NO SOLIDS

... and don't even think of touching the emergency exit door at the back – it's not a toy. We had one young lad bounce out en route to Gladiators. He's now fed through a straw so think on. And I want you back on for midnight. If you're not on, tough because I will go without you.'

He didn't, though. Half one we eventually left, and that was only because I went for a doner kebab and lost my bearings in the short-stay car park.

£

Me and Terry got chatting on the way home when we pulled into some motorway services for a toilet stop and leg stretch. I asked him who were the worst type of passengers he'd had.

'I don't like drunks,' he said. 'I had a load of blokes the other week. Bringing them back from the races. They were like animals. I was halfway up the M6 when I caught one of them having a piss in the middle of the aisle. I got on the mic and said, "Hey, what do you think you're doing?" but he just carried on regardless. So I slammed on the brakes and he shot down the coach at seventy miles an hour, still clutching his dick.

"HEY! HEY! HEY! WHAT ARE YOU DOING?" he was screaming, but I was having none of it. I just pulled onto the hard shoulder and opened the doors.

"Get off."

"SORRY," he said, "I COULDN'T WAIT, MY BACK TEETH WERE FLOATING."

'I said, "Get off my coach, you filthy animal."

'So I watched him get off, and before his piss had the chance to hit the tarmac I shut the doors and drove off. I left him. I left him! He could still be there for all I care. I don't take prisoners in this job.

'Girls can be just as bad, though, if they've had a few drinks. I was taking a load of them home from Take That last summer and they had me stopping every few miles for the toilet. Bladders like fucking egg-cups, women. "We want a wee, we want a wee." I had no choice, so I pulled into the hard shoulder. I let them get off, one by one, waited till they were squatting by the side of the road, knickers down, and I reversed thirty feet and flashed my full beams. They were not amused, not one bit. But you've got to have a laugh. I work hard and I play hard, it's the only way.'

I had to sympathise with Terry the coach driver, as I know exactly how he feels. It's a bugger driving people when they're drunk. You see I don't normally drink so I'm automatically the taxi driver whenever there's a family do or a party. It happens every time. I say I don't mind but it can be a real pain in the arse. Especially when they try and cram that one extra person in.

'Just one more, Peter.'

'I can't. I've got eight in now and it's a five-seater.'

'Please, she's going that way.' Before I know it, they're grabbing her legs and hitching her up into the car.

'Get her ankles! Quick shove her in [slams the door] … she's in, it's all right, she's in.'

'Her dress is caught.'

'Oh bollocks to her dress,' and then they bang on the roof of the car with their fist and off you go.

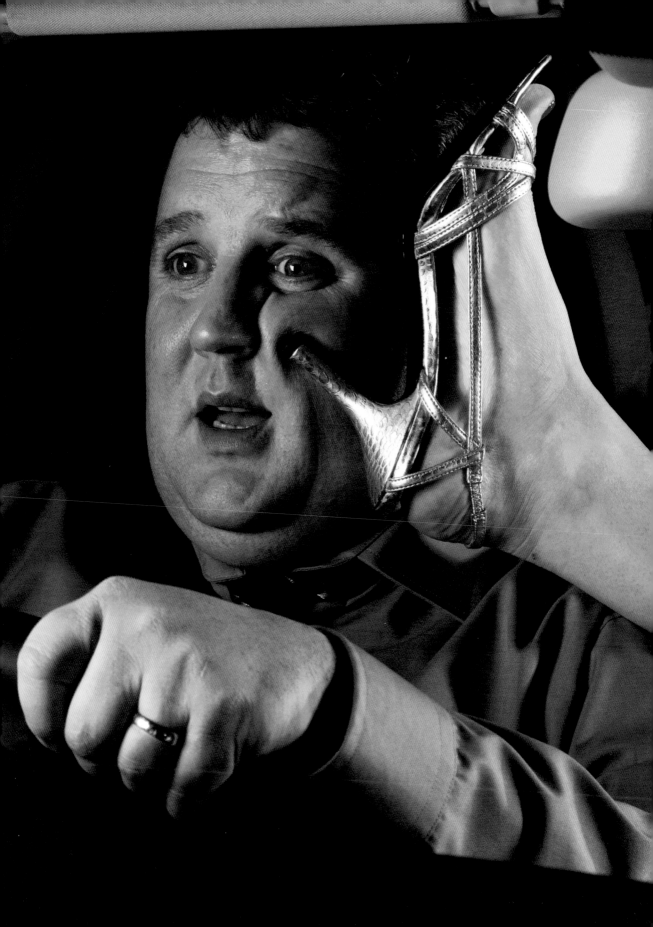

That particular drunken debacle was last New Year's Eve at my cousin's house. It was the night when my uncle Nobhead almost blew himself up with a rocket. Ever since the millennium there's been this fashion in Britain for having fireworks at New Year. I quite like them, and as our house is on a hill we can leg it upstairs at midnight and watch them from the bedroom window. It's a marvellous spectacle, thousands of coloured fireworks exploding across the horizon in unison. Why, even just writing about it brings a tear to my eye – oh no, sorry, my wife's peeling onions, just wait while I move into another room … I can't go in there, they're watching Hole in the Wall, I can't write while that's on. This will have to do. I can't believe I'm sat on the stairs. I hope no one needs to come upstairs. They'll have to climb over me because I'm not moving.

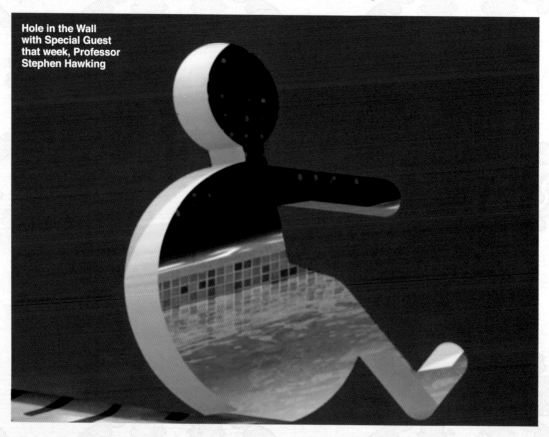

Hole in the Wall with Special Guest that week, Professor Stephen Hawking

I've never been a fan of those do-it-yourself fireworks. Big organised displays are all right, but preferably on the telly so you can turn the sound down and stay warm. I'm talking about those shitty fireworks that parents get on Bonfire Night. My dad always used to pick up a box of No Frills Fireworks on his way home from work. What a rip-off they were. I mean, it's not like you could complain to anybody after they'd gone off, 'cause they'd already gone off.

R Julie and me used to stand inside the house with our cagoules on, watching my dad through the kitchen window. Stumbling around in the darkness with a bucket of sand and a box of Swan Vesta. My mum used to turn the big light off so we could get the 'full effect'.

My dad would pick a coloured firework out of the box and read it out to us, mee-mawing its name to us through the glass. **'THIS ONE'S CALLED THE TORNADO'**, and then he'd give us the thumbs-up.

FIREWORKS

PLEASE READ INSTRUCTIONS INSIDE BEFORE LIGHTING

gpsy

After burying the bottom of the firework in the bucket of sand, he'd nervously crouch down and light it at arm's length, turning away from it and squinting his eyes. As if that would protect him if anything were to go wrong. It's a bit like ducking your head when you drive under a low bridge. What's the point?

My dad was still carrying the mental scars of a Catherine Wheel he'd once nailed to next door's back fence, only for sparks to ignite the creosote and burn the whole lot down before the fire brigade had a chance to arrive. Mr Matey was none too pleased.

As soon as there was a flicker of a spark he was out of there in a flash and had legged it up the back yard and pinned himself up against the kitchen window. Another limp thumbs-up, the anticipation was excruciating. We'd wait and wait and then the volcano would finally erupt. Well, I say erupt. There'd be a flutter of white sparks followed by an ear-piercing screech (throwing Mr Matey's cocker spaniel into a frenzy. It was his own fault, it should have been indoors), then the firework would slowly topple over and that would be that. Crap.

We'd wait and wait … and wait for safety's sake, just in case it decided to reignite, but it didn't. My dad would fumble through the assorted box again and pull another one out, reading its label by torchlight. **'THIS ONE'S CALLED THE VOLCANO-VESUVIUS',** and the same sorry process would start all over again. The names always made me laugh because they tried to create an expectation of excitement which was rarely reflected in what you were about to see. They all appeared to be the same, as far as I could tell. Only the traffic light firework bore any difference to the others. That would start off as an ear-piercing screech and a flutter of green sparks slowly followed by red before it would keel over in exhaustion. What traffic lights do that?

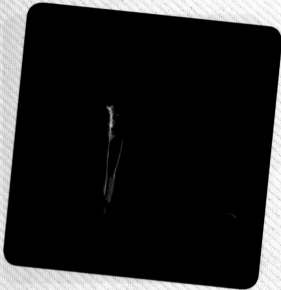

The Volcano

THE TORNADO!

The Whistling Gypsy

175

The only thing I really liked about Bonfire Night was the food and the sparklers. My mum always picked up a pack of sparklers from the newsagent's at the top of the street. We'd light them in between the bars on the gas fire, then run outside as fast as we could where we'd then have forty-two seconds to write our names as many times as we liked before it would take the flesh off our fingers.

As anyone born in the 1970s will know, the cardinal rule was never to pick a sparkler up once it was on the floor. Like the little girl on that public information film that traumatised a generation for life. I can still see her now, screaming and then starting 6 November with her mutilated, bandaged hand held up to the camera. If my dad had managed to wangle some overtime, he'd occasionally splash out on a couple of rockets. He'd

shove each one into a sterilised milk bottle which doubled as a makeshift launcher. But last New Year my uncle Nobhead's rocket was so big, he had to use Nu Fang Dow's washing basket as a launch module.

Every year Nobhead succeeded in dazzling and amazing us with his array of under-the-counter fireworks he'd commandeered from a 'friend' he'd served with in the Falklands conflict. But last year he managed to get his hands on a piece of armoury that would have caused the Taliban to blush.

It was like a scene from The A-Team★ watching him cable-tie the rocket shell into the basket (probably not a good idea after five Jack Daniels and Coke). Everybody gathered by the kitchen window at the back for the annual drunken rendition of 'Auld Lang Syne'.

But my attention was on Uncle Nobhead McNabb as he staggered around the darkened back yard with his enormous rocket. He was slurring a countdown from ten, but tragically the rocket ignited on the count of six and began to spin in several different directions, none of which was up.

Our singing quickly subsided into gasps, as our heads turned (in slow motion) in horror to witness Nobhead's rocket as it toppled over and then suspiciously took aim at the man himself. Nobhead's bloodshot eyes widened in realisation as he hastily turned on a sixpence and tripped over a crate of Newcastle Brown Ale, sending him headfirst over a trellis wall. Narrowly missing him, the rocket then mysteriously spiralled upwards on a right-angle and off into the night sky. It appeared that even the rocket didn't like him. Everybody managed to leg it outside just in time to catch the wake of its explosion. I have to admit, it was a pretty magnificent sight, and the rocket wasn't so bad either.

I was feeling flush and more than a little merry that night; in fact, I feel obliged to confess to you that I had consumed the very legal limit of alcohol on that particular New Year's Eve. Quite shocking, I realise, but now that we're friends I can openly admit to having a cheeky penchant for the occasional tipple of Bailey's. Granted it's more of a dessert than a drink (I'll start Monday), but I find it wets my whistle in more ways than one. In fact, I've even found myself secretly loading it into my coffee during Countdown. Is that a problem?

★ The original series, not that sacrilegious remake with Liam Neeson.

The last and the only time I've ever been officially drunk was on an occasion that anybody with any empathy would understand: my school reunion. There's a perfectly good reason why I've not kept in touch with those people and seeing them again confirmed my suspicions. There's a reason the past has passed and I've always believed that resurrecting it can often be a terrible disappointment.

Someone got in touch with me through Facetube and, as to be expected in this situation, my curiosity got the better of me. So, against my better judgement, I went. I don't think I've ever experienced anything more surreal. It was like a dream. You know the kind of dream where you bore your nearest and dearest to death over breakfast as you regale them with excited tales of the previous night's nocturnal adventures. 'You were there but you had sandbags instead of legs and we were being chased by a sixty-foot Chris de Burgh who was kicking minis over for charity.' They nod politely, as it makes complete sense to you but absolutely none to them. Attending my school reunion was exactly the same.

Exercise

BOOK

Peter Kay

Algebra

3rd Year

Back in the company of friends and acquaintances I hadn't had the pleasure of seeing for over twenty years, I was stunned by how much older, fatter and balder everybody had gotten (and that was just the women). I mean, you know you're getting old when the local lollipop lady was in your class at school.

What tickled me the most was how quickly everybody formed back into the same old groups they were in for every school disco we ever had.

'Hi, good to see you,' came a voice from over my shoulder. I turned to see the familiar face of a boy now a man.

He hugged the life out of me. Lifting me clean off the floor.

'God, it's bloody good to see you,' he bellowed in his thick Bolton accent.

Problem was I couldn't for the life of me remember his name.

'So what have you been up to?'

'Oh nowt much,' he said.

Twenty-years and 'nowt much'.

It was at this point I realised that I was in for a very long night.

I spied a gaggle of nuns over in the corner and was

immediately gripped by a feeling of fear and dread that I hadn't experienced since I first inhaled Tipp-Ex in third year and got suspended for patting a teacher's hump.

I may have been delirious but I genuinely saw it as a show of affection.

When I first found out we had nuns at school, I thought it was going to be all singing and hiding Nazis, but I was gravely mistaken. All I got was the fear of God and a terror of algebra that was still plaguing me at the start of this book.

I'd like to tell you that it was great to see the sisters again, but I'd quickly have to follow it up with an act of contrition because I'd be lying through my teeth. There they were in all of their holy glory and they hadn't changed a bit—still as old and miserable as ever. It's common knowledge that nuns have no sense of humour, nun whatsoever. (Sorry, that was pretty lame.)

And it wasn't for want of trying to get them to crack the occasional smile. Every year we'd send them a Valentine's card from Jesus Christ. Strategically posting it through the convent door in the middle of the night. But we got nothing, not even a titter. And it wasn't just thrown together; we used to spend hours on the verses. 'Roses are Red, Violets are Blue, Sugar Is

Sweet, I Died for You': that was one of my personal favourites.

We even went to the time and the trouble to sneak into the hall before Easter assembly one year, to dress up the crucifix on stage in a body-warmer and Afro wig. But again, when they opened the curtains, nothing. The nuns just stood there with their mouths open. Well, the ones that could stand did. The rest were

just quickly wheeled out of the hall with oxygen. Either way, humour was completely lost on the nuns.

Sister Sledge was the headmistress at our school. She was lost in music, caught in a trap, no turning back. She used to smoke roll-ups. She once summoned all the boys into the assembly hall because someone had thrown a shatterproof ruler at Carol Farrell. 'If it had been an inch lower it would have been instant death,' she screamed at us. Instant death? From a shatterproof ruler? Come off it they're only 30 cm long and so what if they bend. Let me ask you, was there a time before shatterproof rulers existed? Why were they invented? There must have been a reason. Were rulers blowing up in kids' faces or something like that? Was there a national outcry? 'We've got to get our rulers shatterproofed, and quick!' Whatever happened, I'm pretty sure they weren't to blame for any 'instant deaths'. If they were, surely the powers that be would have organised some kind of stationery armistice. People would be queuing up all over Britain, stood outside police stations nervously clutching shatterproof rulers, protractors and compasses.

'When I find out who did it,' Sister Sledge said, gesturing her crooked finger in my general direction, 'I'm going to drag them up on that stage in assembly and bang them in front of everybody.' I thought, No, she can't do that, surely she'd be breaking a pretty big vow?

We didn't just have nuns teaching us, thank the Lord. We had real teachers too. We had humans. I wonder if there are any teachers reading this right now? If you are, please go eesy on the spullings. I'm doing my bust.

My favourite teachers at school used to be the ones with amnesia.

'Who do you think you are? Who do you think you're talking to? How old are you? Where should you be? Do you know who I am?'

And I was a particular fan of the completely idiotic things teachers used to say. Things like: 'Silence when you're talking to me', 'Don't come in here and start shouting the odds', 'Act your age, not your shoe size', 'Put your pens down and watch the blackboard while I go through it.' I'd be sat watching the board, waiting for a teacher to charge through the wall.

Another one was when a class was chatting and the teacher would resort to the old favourite. 'Keep talking, that's it, keep talking, because the longer you talk, the longer you'll stay. I don't care what time I go home.'

A quarter to nine we kept him till. He was desperate to leave. 'Erm ... I'm supposed to be going for a meal with my wife.'

'No,' I said, 'bollocks to you, you said you weren't bothered. We're happy here, I'm taping Taggart – I'll watch it when I get home.'

Did you ever try and blind a teacher with your watch? We used to do it all the time. In fact, if there'd been an O level in it I'd have passed with flying colours. It used to drive the teachers mad.

'I know exactly who it is.'

No he didn't, because he couldn't see a damn thing. Another even better one was to try and burn a hole in the front of his pants. If everybody focused on his balls you could get his groin smouldering in practically no time at all. That got us through many a dull lesson and always came in handy with supply teachers. They were only there for the day. We managed to get this one poor guy's chinos smoking.

Actual black smoke emanating from his crotch area. Teamwork; it almost brought a tear to my eye and both of his — well, until the fire bell went off and we ended up in the car park.

At the end of a lesson I always wanted to be one of the first out of the classroom. I'd start discreetly packing up all my stuff about five minutes before the bell went. I'd slowly put everything back in my pencil case while still pretending to carry on writing with my imaginary pen. The teacher couldn't see because usually there was someone sat in front. So I would mime away to my heart's content, looking all interested and engaged in what they were saying. Next, I'd slide my coat on from the back of my chair. Delicately and quietly pulling the zip up over each tooth until it reached the top.

Then I'd start to lift my bum off the chair and edge it towards the door with one eye on the clock. Just the last few seconds now as I hovered in mid-air, poised with one hand clutching the strap of my bag, the other still miming a pen. Then 'RING-RING-RING-RING', and thirty of us would all be wedged in the door in unison.

'RIGHT BACK, BACK, BACK, BACK, BACK,
EVERYBODY BACK IN YOUR SEATS NOW!! That bell is
for me not for you. That bell is a signal for ME! So I can then tell
YOU! When you can go!' There'd then be another huge pause as
everybody froze holding their breath. 'Right, now you can go.'

Power-mad they were, teachers. They loved it. Mr Brice was
the worst one for that at our school. He used to be obsessed with
straight lines. We would literally spend hours in the playground
lining up while he measured us with a piece of tape.

'Jackson step in ... Halliwell in ... Kay, you're still sticking
out boy ...'

There'd be another long dramatic pause, eventually followed
by, 'Right, that's straight, now in you go.' Then we all immediately
had to turn right in order to enter the building. The man was
nuts. No, seriously, when I think back to it all now I genuinely
think he had a screw loose. He once took us all out on a
geography field trip to a graveyard to visit his wife, I swear
to God. We just went along with it but, looking back on it now,
that's not the work of a sane man. He sat there at the graveside
sobbing while we were playing army around the headstones.
We didn't know what else to do. Then he got the hump with

us and literally left us there. We had to walk five miles home in the rain.

Mr Brice was at the school reunion. I saw him leaning on the piano in the corner, still sporting his hump. I felt like snorting some Tipp-Ex and giving him a squeeze for old times' sake, but he was never a fan of my work.

'See me' was permanently scrawled at the bottom of any of my homework he'd marked.

'You think you're the clown ... is that what you're going to be when you grow up, Kay, a comedian? I tell you where you're going to end up, the thick table. Go on, get your stuff and get on the thick table until you learn to behave.'

We used to have a thick table in our class at school. Now when I say thick table I don't mean literally a 'thick' table, like a giant oak dining room table from King Arthur's court. I mean a table for thickos, as Mr Brice liked to call them. Basically, the academically challenged members of our classroom community, and as a punishment you were forced to sit with them.

How cruel is that? (I'm referring to the people of the thick table, not the having to sit with them part, although at the time that was a bit of a bummer.) What astonishes me is that we're not talking about the 1950's. This was just over twenty years ago. People would shudder in disgust at such an act of discrimination in this current world of political correctness. You'd never get away with it today. There was no diagnosis of ADHD or dyslexia; they just slapped you across the back of the head and stuck you on the thick table. 'If you're going to act thick then I'll put you with thick.'

I mean, realistically, what chance did those kids stand? No wonder most of them either got sent down, ended up collecting trolleys or, worse, went into politics. I was lucky to get out of there alive.

Jason Patel, he was on the thick table for the crime of being born with a lazy eye. The last time I saw him he was pairing socks for the mentally ill. Jason was permanently on the thick table as far back as I can remember; in fact, I'm sure he arrived in reception carrying a collapsible thick table.

WHAT'S THIS??
An Austin Allegro Sister.

Thomas Hodgekiss was incarcerated on the thick table for the supposed sin of swallowing bubbly. Before he knew it he had a fight-sized crowd gathered round him in the playground. Pandemonium and hysteria ensued, with screams of 'Quick, get him to the nurse before it wraps around his insides and kills him.' We were even forced to endure the obligatory impressions of the emergency services as a couple of kids charged around the yard 'nee-nawing' and 'sirening' to the annoyance of many. With the clock ticking, Thomas was whisked off to hospital in the back of the school nurse's Austin Allegro.

For that particular mishap he was quarantined on the thick table for the rest of the year ... oh, and he also had a club foot.

Then there was Theresa Crankfist, with snot bubbles as big as tennis balls exploding with a volcanic ferocity. Lord above, now there's an image burned into my retinas for eternal damnation. Even the very thought of her name quickly conjures up that familiar aroma of warm wet piss, drying slowly next to a radiator. Unfortunately I sat next to Theresa for most of my academic life. And on the odd occasion when I violently jolt out of my dreams and sit bolt upright in fear, you can bet your sweet arse that Theresa's played a part in it somewhere.

I find it fascinating and maybe a bit worrying that those people have stayed embedded in my mind for all this time. They even came back to haunt me when my wife and I were picking baby names,

'If it's a girl what about Theresa?'

Suddenly the image of Theresa Crankfist wiping pale green mucus from her eyebrows appeared before me and sent a shiver down my back.

'NO!' I shouted. 'The child will be cursed.'

One of the activities I used to love at school was when we

got to watch telly once a week. Two prefects would wheel in this enormous TV on massive legs. I can't convey to you how huge it was. It was even bigger to a classroom full of children; we used to have to sit up like meerkats in order to watch it. It once had a video in a lock box that'd been nicked and a remote control on a wire. I can still see Sister Matic stood on her desk clutching the wire aerial in her hand and waving it around over her head whilst asking us, 'Can you see? Is there a picture now? ... What about now?'

I was never a fan of PE at school. I can imagine your astonishment, but it just never did it for me. I wasn't a fan of any kind of sport. Perhaps that was because I had two nicknames as a rule: Fat Bastard and Shift. Children can be so kind. As a result, I never saw the point of Physical Education; I couldn't understand how you were supposed to become physically educated at our school when all they used to make us do was walk back and forth along an upturned gym bench and then do a forward roll.

Then Sister O'Mercy would shout, 'ALL CHANGE

And we'd have to quickly leg it over to the ropes before another group got there first. 'The ropes! Quick, get on the ropes get on the ropes ... Shit! It's not fair this, Sister, they've been on the ropes twice now. While we're still stuck balancing on this upturned gym bench?'

Occasionally I'd lie and tell them I'd forgotten my PE kit but that would backfire. Sister O'Mercy would just point at an old clothes bin in the corner of the changing room and shout, 'Get something out of there.'

So I'd still end up walking along on the upturned gym bench, only now I'd be wearing a fencing mask and a netball skirt.

Because I was a child of the bigger boned variety my mum prescribed packed lunches for most of my school life in an effort to keep my weight down. It probably would have worked if she hadn't given me a daily dose of two Spam sandwiches, a Munch Bunch yoghurt, with a packet of Salt 'n' Shake and a Highland Toffee all neatly jammed inside a Miami Vice lunchbox.

On Mondays I used to get a bit of angel cake or a slice of Madeira wrapped up in foil that was left over from a Sunday afternoon after watching The Love Boat and Bullseye.

My mum also used to give me a beaker of orange cordial with a piece of clingfilm stretched under the lid so it wouldn't spill in my bag on the way to school. But it always did, and by the time I arrived my textbooks would be sodden. That's why I used to have to back my books in wallpaper. Wood chip, Anaglypta, Razzle – basically whatever I could get my hands on. I didn't waste my evenings growing up. That actually became quite fashionable for a few years. 'Mum, could you get me that roll of wood chip from the side of the wardrobe?'

My dad always used to keep off-cuts of wallpaper 'just in case', which would be wedged behind wardrobes and cupboards all over the house. He used to save off-cuts from carpets too,

would
nion.
eason
 with
them
cions.
t has
ieved
en be
ent.
ith me
s to be
on, my
of me.
better
't think
nything
dream.
dream
earest
over
them
the
urnal
but

TV STARS

WHO IS THIS???

Crockett and Tubbs, Sister.

but that's a whole other story. (I'll save that for Book Four.)

   It was common for people to slag off school dinners, but I always loved them. I'd often scoff my packed lunch and then eat my friends' leftovers (it's a disease quite common with insecure fat people). In fact I thought they were great long before Jamie Oliver stuck his nose in and ruined them for everybody. I'd never even seen a turkey's twizzler until he rocked up. There was nothing wrong with the food at our school as far as I could see.

We ate like kings: chips and beans, chips and peas, chips and gravy, fish fingers on Friday with smiley potato faces. Truly a balanced diet if ever I saw one. Though some girl would always fall with her dinner walking back to her seat and Sister Scissors would end up with beans down her vestments, at least once a fortnight. We'd all bang on the tables and cheer, didn't you know, it's a British custom when anybody drops some crockery or breaks a glass. The nuns would try to calm us down. 'Keep moving, there's nothing to see.'

When people were sick at school the nuns used to put sawdust on it. What was all that about?

Bloody sawdust on vomit. 'Keep eating, there's nothing to see.'

'Of course there's something to see,' I'd protest. 'That girl's throwing up shavings. What is she, some kind of carpenter's daughter? She's clearly a freak, she should be on Embarrassing Bodies.'

The nuns were still sprinkling sawdust on the floor at the school reunion. By half ten, anybody who was still there was either drunk or throwing up and Sister R Doin It was desperately chasing after them round the dance floor with a bucket of sawdust. I'd had one too many Bailey's and found myself on the karaoke with my old mate from the thick table, Theresa Crankfist. Both of us were giving a heartfelt rendition of the old school classic 'Bump n' Grind'. Theresa was off her tits, pole-dancing with the crucifix, while I searched for an Afro wig for old times' sake. Sister Sledge was losing her mind, 'Get them off the stage. I'll kill them, I'll fecking kill them! Where's my shatterproof ruler?'

SEE ME AGAIN !!!!

3/10

203

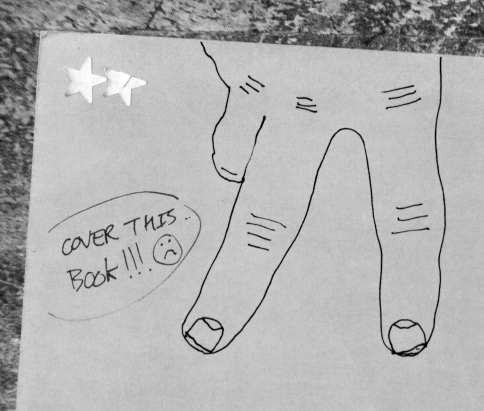

I eventually got home at a quarter past three. The least said the better. I have to admit that I was more than a little worse for wear. I staggered upstairs into the bedroom and undressed myself by the light of the charging mobiles. Then, as I was gently tiptoeing to the bog, I went arse over tit on a pair of shoes, landed face down in a pile of wire coat hangers and knocked my brand-new tooth out.

Good Night Vienna!

Photography © Matt Squire

Illustrations © Bill Greenhead

Additional stock photography:
Alamy
Author's personal collection
BBC Picture Library
Stuart Conway/Camera Press, London
Channel 4/Ken Loveday
Endemol UK
Getty Images
istockphoto
PA Photos
Rex Features
Rosemaryconley.com
Shutterstock
Trevillion Images/Catherine Forrest
Unilever

'Carrie' illustration © Roger Stine for 'Cinéfantastique' magazine, 1976
Still from 'The Cannonball Run' © Twentieth Century Fox/Golden
Harvest/Ronald Grant Archive
Still from 'Charlie & the Chocolate Factory' © Wolper/Warner Bros./
The Kobal Collection
Stills from firework safety public information film © COI/BFI
Still from 'Marathon Man' © Paramount/The Kobal Collection
Draught excluders courtesy of Refab/www.refab.co.uk

Every reasonable effort has been made to trace copyright holders,
but if there are any errors or omissions, Hodder & Stoughton will
be pleased to insert the appropriate acknowledgement in any
subsequent printings or editions.

The Publishers would like to thank everyone who has contributed
to the production of this book.

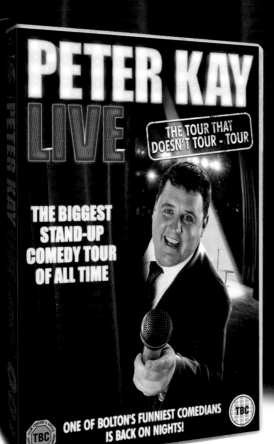

PETER KAY
LIVE

THE TOUR THAT DOESN'T TOUR - TOUR

"HILARIOUS, SPECTACULAR AND HUGELY ENTERTAINING"

"A NATIONAL COMIC TREASURE"

Coming to DVD and Blu-ray 7th November 2011